Embroidered Treasures for Silk Ribbon

BOOK 1

Embroidered Treasures for Silk Ribbon

Book 1

Helen Dafter

SALLY MILNER PUBLISHING

First published in 1999 by
Sally Milner Publishing Pty Ltd
PO Box 2104
Bowral NSW 2576
Australia

© Helen Dafter 1999

Design and page layout by Anna Warren, Warren Ventures P/L
Photography by Andrew Elton
Styling by Regina Walters
Edited by Kathryn Lamberton, Bridging the Gap, Sydney
Printed and bound in Hong Kong

National Library of Australia
Cataloguing in Publication Data

Dafter, Helen
    Embroidered treasures for silk ribbon

    Includes index
    ISBN 1 86351 240 3.

    1. Silk ribbon embroidery. 2. Ribbon work I. Title
    (Series : Milner craft series)

    746.44

Contents

Acknowledgements 7

Materials and Techniques 8
   Ribbons 8
   Storage of ribbons 8
   Stranded threads 9
   Needles 9
   Scissors 9
   Fabric marking pens 10
   Embroidery hoops 10
   Fabric choice 11
   Pretreatment of fabric 11
   Transferring designs 12

A Guide to Stitching 13
   Threading the needle 13
   Knotting the ribbon 13
   Maintaining the right tension 13
   Working parts of flowers in order 14
   Creating perspective 14
   Ending off 16

The Stitches 17
   Basic ribbon stitch 17
   Extended ribbon stitch 18
   Couched ribbon stitch 18
   Side ribbon stitch 19
   French knot 19
   Loop stitch 20
   Fly stitch 20
   Straight stitch 21

Spiderweb or woven rose   21

Stem stitch   22

Pistil stitch   23

Feather stitch   23

Formation of flower buds   24

Formation of spider web   25

Painted Backgrounds   26

Introduction to the Projects   29

Index to the Projects   30

Stockists   102

Acknowledgements

My family, my friends, my publisher, my suppliers and many fellow embroiderers have all contributed to this series of books in many and varied ways.

I am indebted to Sally Milner Publishing Pty Ltd for having faith in my projects and for managing to retain their sense of humour during the various editorial stages. They were always available for testing out my ideas and aspirations.

A large amount of credit for the text of this book must be given to the many embroiderers whom I have had the pleasure of meeting during the last few years. It is only through discussion with people who have similar interests that it is possible to gauge where explanation may be required by the reader and the extent of instructions and hints that should be included. Not only have I provided projects which have given me a great deal of pleasure to make, but I have also included information concerning the craft of silk ribbon embroidery. I hope that within these pages you will find what you need to ensure the success of your silk ribbon embroidery projects.

I would also like to thank my suppliers — an ever increasing number — for their advice, their help and their generosity which has made my task much easier and more enjoyable.

Many family members and friends, whether embroiderers or not, have also helped me along the way: the embroiderers because they have allowed me the luxury of using them as sounding boards for ideas and inspiration; the non-embroiderers simply because I enjoy their company and return to the task of producing a new project or design refreshed by their friendship alone. I gratefully acknowledge their collective assistance.

Lastly, but most importantly, a special thank you to my husband, Glenn, and my children, Naomi, Matthew and Brian. They rarely contribute in any practical sense to the content, but their continued love and support is tangible and irreplaceable.

Happy stitching! HELEN DAFTER, 1999

Materials and
Techniques

RIBBONS

Pure silk ribbon in a variety of widths, the most common being 2mm, 4mm and 7mm, has been used for all the projects, although a nylon ribbon known as Spark Organdy has sometimes been used to fill in background areas. This ribbon is available in a variety of widths and a number of colours. It has quite a sparkle and is therefore useful for adding interest to a project.

Currently, plain-dyed silk ribbon is available in 186 colours and five different widths. Pure silk embroidery ribbon is becoming increasingly available in what is known as hand-dyed or overdyed ranges, both from Australia and overseas, in an increasing number of colours. Some of the ranges include several different widths of ribbon; others do not.

Several of the projects included in this book have been worked exclusively in overdyed ribbons because, through the subtle variations in tone and colour, they help to add dimension to the work, bringing the embroidery to life. When using these ribbons, I do not cut different lengths and shadings of the ribbons; instead I work systematically along the length of ribbon until the project is complete.

STORAGE OF RIBBON

Pure silk ribbons can become tangled and damaged very easily. Effective storage of these ribbons will not only ensure that they are cared for but will also make the selection of colours much easier. Preferably, they need to be wound on a circular object, such as a cotton reel, a lunchwrap cylinder with slits cut to fasten the ends of the ribbon, or the central cardboard cylinder of a fax paper roll. If they are wound onto a cardboard floss bobbin, you will find that they become creased at regular intervals and will require ironing prior to use.

STRANDED THREADS

Rajmahal stranded art silk has been used exclusively for the embroideries in this book because I feel that the lustre of this thread and the colours available complement the silk ribbon perfectly and bring a richness to this type of embroidery. Rajmahal is a six-stranded thread available in an 8m skein. A single thread has been used at all times unless otherwise indicated in the design notes. Stranded cotton in appropriate colours may be substituted to match the silk ribbon used.

NEEDLES

The correct choice of needle type and size is critical to the success of your ribbon embroidery work. A chenille needle is essential because it protects the ribbon as it is drawn through the fabric. It has a large diameter shaft, a large eye and a sharp point and is available in a number of sizes. The shaft of this needle forces the fibres of the fabric apart, allowing the easy passage of the silk ribbon through the fabric. The sharp point of the needle pierces the ribbon with minimal damage when doing ribbon stitch, a stitch peculiar to ribbon embroidery. The needle size chosen depends on the width of the ribbon used, and the needle chosen determines how the stitch will 'sit' in the space made by the shaft of the needle. If a large needle is used with a narrow embroidery ribbon, the stitch may not sit neatly on the surface of the fabric.

The following chart may help with needle selection:

Size 18 — 7mm and 4mm silk ribbons, Spark Organdy ribbons

Size 20 — 4mm ribbon

Size 22 — 2mm ribbon

Size 24 — 2mm ribbon

A Size 13 chenille needle is also available. This is quite useful if you are using some of the wider silk ribbons available, as well as other embroidery ribbons, particularly on finer fabrics.

SCISSORS

A sharp pair of embroidery scissors is essential for cutting silk ribbon into workable lengths and snipping any long threads or ribbons from the back of your work.

Remember to protect your scissors when you place them in your work basket to ensure that the ends stay sharp.

FABRIC MARKING PENS

There are a number of fabric marking pens available and it is easy to find one suitable for the type of fabric you are working on. My preference is a fine-line, water-soluble blue marking pen which allows you to mark designs on almost any fabric. These marks can be removed after the embroidery is complete by gently dabbing them with a cotton bud dipped in cold water and allowing the fabric and embroidery to air dry. If traces of the blue marking pen are still visible — as they are occasionally — simply repeat the process until the marks disappear. A white water-soluble marking pen, which works in the same way, is also available. This is used for marking dark fabrics.

Air-erasable pens, which react to the amount of moisture in the atmosphere are also handy, though the marks created by this type of pen will disappear in varying amounts of time and may not be there when you are ready to embroider.

If you are apprehensive about using a marking pen on a piece of expensive or delicate fabric, test it first on an unobtrusive edge of the fabric to ensure that the marking lines can be easily removed.

EMBROIDERY HOOPS

I find it essential to work my designs in an appropriately sized embroidery hoop. By working in a hoop, I am able to maintain an even tension on the fabric and to concentrate on the tension of the stitches I am creating. I have a number of hoops in a variety of materials and sizes.

My preference is a good quality plastic hoop as this tends to grip the fabric, as well as preventing 'retensioning' of the fabric. As a general rule, choose a hoop that fits outside the perimeter of the embroidery you have chosen to avoid 'bruising' completed stitches.

It is a good idea to leave excess fabric around the embroidered area so that you can choose from a range of hoop sizes. If you decide on this option, you will need to trim the fabric to size once the embroidery is complete. If an item is too small to fit into the hoop you have available, you can stitch some waste fabric to the edges of your embroidery fabric to enable it to fit the hoop. If you are embroidering an unusual shape, mark the shape on the fabric but don't cut it out until the embroidery is complete. By retaining the fabric surround, you should be able to find a suitable hoop to use.

You may also find that you need to move your hoop around to work a particular design. If this is the case, it is advisable to leave out sections of the design until other areas have been completed, to avoid damaging those smaller areas. Occasionally, several flowers will need to be finished after the fabric has been removed from the hoop.

Tip: Once you have placed the fabric in the hoop, use four safety pins to hold the folded fabric in the corners out of the way of your working area. This will avoid accidently stitching the excess fabric around the outside of the hoop to the back of your work.

Fabric choice

I recommend following this general rule when choosing fabric for an embroidery: if you can pull the needle easily through the fabric, then you can embroider on it. Obviously, some materials are more suitable than others. For example, sheer or lightweight fabrics require more attention when finishing off at the rear of the work than heavier fabrics, otherwise ribbon ends and threads will be visible through the fabric.

The projects in this book have been worked on a variety of fabrics, including cotton, silk and pure wool. If you are in doubt as to the suitability of a particular fabric, test it by drawing a needle through the fabric. If prepainting is required, test a small section with a wash of paint.

Pretreatment of fabric

Generally, fabric for embroidery should not be prewashed. This is particularly important if you are preparing a painted backgound for your embroidery design.

If using a lightweight fabric, such as silk, use a flexible iron-on interfacing such as Whisperweft or Armorweft. Once the interfacing has been ironed onto the back of the fabric, machine neaten the edges to prevent excess fraying which can occur through continuous handling during the embroidery stage. The use of a suitable interfacing will also allow you to thread the silk ribbon between the two layers of fabric to end off, rather than using a thread to stitch the tail of the ribbon in place or tying a knot — always risky as you might pull and distort the previous stitch.

Transferring designs

There are several methods for transferring a design onto your fabric. Below are the two which I prefer.

1. Lightbox

If you have a lightbox, this is the easiest way to transfer a design onto a lightweight fabric. Simply tape the design sheet onto the surface of the lightbox, place your fabric on top and, using a fabric marking pen, transfer the design to your fabric. This method is not suitable for thicker fabrics such as blanketing and velvet. You can also improvise by making use of a sunlit window in a similar way.

2. Bridal tulle or netting

If the project requires a thicker fabric, use the following method to transfer your design. Place the design sheet on a flat surface. Then lay a piece of greaseproof paper over the design sheet and pin the tulle to the layers below. (The greasproof paper will protect the design sheet from marks made during the next step.) Using a permanent black marking pen, such as a laundry marker, trace the major design elements, such as stem and flower placement, onto the tulle. Don't draw every leaf and petal as this will be too confusing. Once the pen marks are quite dry, pin the tulle in place on your fabric and use a fabric marking pen to draw over the black lines and through the tulle to transfer the stem lines and flower positions onto your fabric.

A Guide to Stitching

Threading the needle

A technique known as 'locking on' is used when embroidering with pure silk ribbon. The end of the ribbon is threaded through the eye of the needle, the point of the needle is inserted approximately 6mm (¼") from the end of the ribbon and the tail of the ribbon is then pulled. This 'locks' the ribbon to the eye of the needle.

Knotting the ribbon

Not quite a knot — more of a loop — is made in the tail of the ribbon to prevent it being drawn through to the front of the fabric. The ribbon is locked onto the needle as described above, the tail of the ribbon is held and the needle is passed through the ribbon twice, approximately 6mm (¼") apart and the same distance from the end of the ribbon. The needle is then pulled through the ribbon, the resulting loop at the tail end of the ribbon being sufficient to keep the ribbon at the back of your embroidery. This loop is quite flat and will prevent excess bulk at the back of your work.

Alternatively, you can tie a simple knot to start the ribbon off, or you can leave a tail of ribbon to be stitched down with thread after several stitches have been completed.

Maintaining the right tension

This is generally known as 'letting the ribbon do the work for you'!

The most common mistake is pulling the stitches too tightly. This gives the impression that they have been formed with multiple strands of embroidery thread rather than silk ribbon.

If you have used an embroidery hoop and chosen the right needle, and the stitches still don't look right, it may be because you are pulling the stitches too tightly or because the ribbon is not being encouraged to lie flat against the fabric before you complete each stitch.

The most common stitch I use is basic ribbon stitch and the difference between pulling it too tightly and not pulling it tightly enough is minimal.

If you tend to pull your stitches too tightly, try putting your finger over the stitch at the point where you insert the needle through the ribbon to pull the ribbon through to the back of your work. This will prevent the stitch pulling and distorting.

Always ensure that the ribbon is lying as flat as possible — with no folds — before completing a stitch. It is almost impossible to adjust the ribbon after a stitch has been completed. Run the shaft of the needle down the width of the ribbon to encourage it to lie flat.

If these few helpful tips are followed, the width of the ribbon will do most of the work for you and you will enjoy your embroidery much more.

If you still manage to pull the occasional stitch too tightly, pull it even tighter, taking care not to damage the previous stitch, and work another ribbon stitch over the top of the pulled one to camouflage the unacceptably tight stitch. By doing this, you can avoid taking the stitch out and still achieve a very pleasing result.

WORKING PARTS OF FLOWERS IN ORDER

Included in the text for each of the projects is a list of the flowers featured. I have listed the components of each of the flowers in the order in which they should be worked.

CREATING PERSPECTIVE

1. Incorporate a painted background

Preparing a painted background prior to working any embroidery significantly enhances the depth in the completed project. Even a one-colour background adds to the creation of depth. It also means that less embroidery has to be worked as less colour will be visible through the stitching.

2. Add a feature

Including a simple feature such as a picket fence, a gate or a pathway enhances the depth of the image. Drawing or painting the feature will increase the perception of depth even more.

3. Use different ribbon colours

If darker, richer colours of ribbon are used in the foreground and lighter, softer colours in the background, this will help to create additional depth.

4. Change ribbon widths

As with ribbon colour, ribbon width can also be used for significant visual effect. Narrow ribbons are best reserved for background areas, while wider ribbons increase the sense of depth when used in the foreground.

5. Use different types of ribbon

There are several different types of embroidery ribbon available and one which significantly enhances a landscape-type embroidery is a nylon ribbon known as Spark Organdy. This is available in different widths and a number of colours. It is sheer and is extremely useful for creating dimension, allowing subtle background features, stems, flowers and so on to show through the ribbon.

Rose bud with calyx from thread

6. Use perspective stitching

Including flowers at different angles — front on, from the side or from unusual perspectives — will also increase the depth and interest in an embroidery. While the stitches used to create them may be the same, the careful positioning of the stitches will create the visual difference.

Rose bud with calyx from ribbon

Side view rose

Flower bud

Larger flower bud

Full flower

Flower at an angle

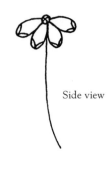

Side view

ENDING OFF

To end off a tail of ribbon after embroidering, simply thread it carefully under the completed stitches and cut away the leftover ribbon, or carefully stitch the end in place using a complementary thread. I find either technique quite successful. Generally, the amount of use an item will have determines which technique I adopt. If it will be used regularly, I would suggest stitching the end of the ribbon in place.

For many of the projects included in this book, interfacing has been used behind the embroidery to give stability to the fabric. If this is the case, the ribbon can be threaded between the fabric and the interfacing and the end buried between these two layers.

The Stitches

Many of the stitches used in ribbon embroidery are formed in the same way as similar stitches for stranded cotton embroidery, with one exception. Ribbon stitch and the variations to this stitch have been developed specially.

If you have a basic understanding of traditional embroidery stitches, then you will have no trouble in interpreting the designs in the projects contained in this book.

Basic ribbon stitch is the most common stitch that I use and it is worthwhile taking the time to practise this stitch before attempting a project.

Basic Ribbon Stitch

1   Draw the ribbon through the fabric at A. You may need to run the shaft of your needle along the length of the ribbon to ensure that it is lying flat against the fabric.

2   Put the point of the needle through the middle of the ribbon, about 8–10mm from the start of the stitch, at B.

3   Gently pull the needle through the ribbon and fabric and continue to pull until the edges of the ribbon curl in at the tip to form a neat, petal-like point.

4   Move onto the beginning of your next stitch, or fasten off.

Note: Care·must be taken not to pull the ribbon too far towards the end of the stitch formation as this will cause the ribbon to fold in on itself and the full effect of the stitch will be lost. You might find it useful to put your thumb or fingernail over the stitch as you pull the ribbon to ensure that you do not pull it too far.

It is easy to vary the effect created with this simple stitch by adjusting the length and tension of the ribbon before piercing it with the needle.

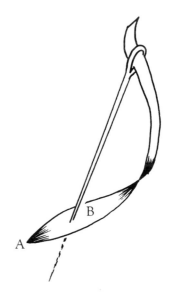

Extended Ribbon Stitch

This is formed in the same way as basic ribbon stitch, but the stitch is worked in varying lengths as required. On an item of heavy wear, a fine row of stitching can be worked down the centre of the stitch if desired. This can also be done to represent the central vein of a leaf, as well as to ensure that the stitch remains in place and does not get caught.

Couched Ribbon Stitch

This stitch is often worked in conjunction with extended ribbon stitch to create the strap-like foliage of different flower groups.

1   Start the stitch as you would for basic ribbon stitch, at A.

2   Determine the length of ribbon required and hold it flat against the fabric.

3   Work 2–3 small stitches in a complementary colour of stranded thread across the width of ribbon at B to couch it in place on the surface.

4   Fold the ribbon over these stitches to hide them.

5   Complete the ribbon stitch at C using the method described for basic ribbon stitch.

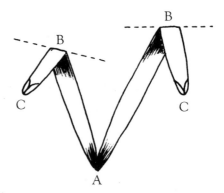

The vein detail may also be added, as described above, if this stitch is being worked on an item of heavy wear.

Side Ribbon Stitch

This is a useful variation on the basic ribbon stitch which allows you to form a slanted ribbon stitch. Simply place the needle through either edge of the ribbon, rather than through the middle of the ribbon, to encourage the ribbon to lean in this direction.

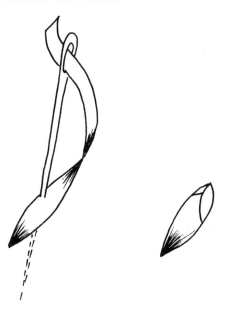

French Knot

1   Draw the ribbon through the fabric at A, with the needle facing away from the fabric.

2   Twist the ribbon around the needle once, stand the needle upright and insert the point of the needle back into the fabric at B, as close to A as possible.

3   Pull the twisted ribbon around the needle until it is quite firm but not too tight as this will prevent you pulling the needle through the fabric.

4   Pull the needle through to the back of the fabric. (Applying tension to the ribbon before pulling the needle through to the back of the fabric will ensure even-sized French knots.)

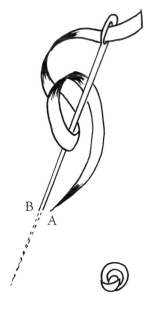

Loop Stitch

1   Draw the ribbon through the fabric, ensuring that it is as flat as possible against the fabric.

2   Turn it back on itself and complete a ribbon stitch slightly above the beginning of the stitch.

3   Use several small stitches in stranded thread to 'couch' the underside of the loop in place. This will prevent the loop from distorting if it is caught.

Fly Stitch

1   Draw thread through fabric at A.

2   Reinsert at B, emerge at C.

3   The resulting 'V' is held in place by reinserting the needle to form a small holding stitch. This can be lengthened to create the stem of a bud.

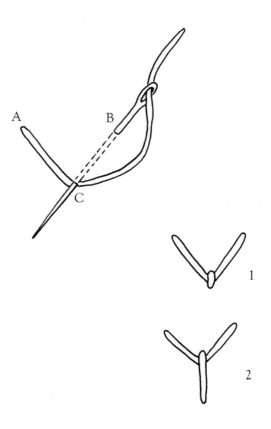

Variations to the length of the
holding stitch to complete
the stem of a bud etc.

Straight Stitch

This stitch is most often worked in stranded cotton, in combination with fly stitch, to add details or stems.

1   Insert needle through fabric at A, making sure that the ribbon is lying as flat as possible.

2   Reinsert at B.

3   Fasten off at back of work or work next stitch.

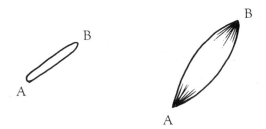

Spiderweb or Woven Rose

1   With 2 strands of a thread in the same colour as the ribbon chosen for the rose, work, the 5 spokes of the web using a fly stitch with an extended tail to form a 'Y' and straight stitches for D-E and F-E. Anchor the thread securely. The spokes must be an even length and evenly spaced.

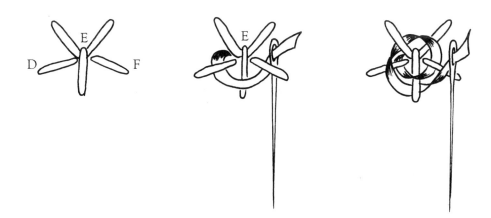

2   Draw the ribbon through the fabric as shown near the centre of the spokes. Reverse the needle and weave the eye of the needle, with the ribbon attached, under and over alternate spokes until all the spokes are covered. (By weaving with the eye of the needle instead of the point, you will ensure that the point of the needle does not catch and pull ribbon that is already woven into place.)

3   Allow each subsequent round of ribbon to sit next to the one before it. Avoid pulling too tightly as this will result in a bulky rose. Allowing the ribbon to twist and fold as you weave will create a very natural-looking rose.

4   Return the ribbon to the back of the work and fasten off.

The size of the rose will vary in accordance with the size of the initial web, the width of ribbon used, the number of times the ribbon is woven around the spokes and the tension of the ribbon as it is woven.

A French knot in a darker shade may be worked first at the centre of the spokes to form the centre of the rose. For a larger rose, a triangle of French knots may be worked at the centre.

Stem Stitch

This stitch is most often worked in stranded thread to create the stems and branches of various flowers.

1   Begin at A, reinsert at B and emerge at C.

2   Repeat until stem is the desired length and shape.

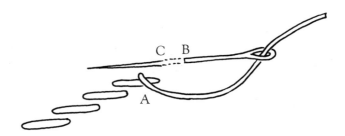

Pistil Stitch

This stitch is formed in the same way as a French knot, but instead of inserting the needle very close to where it emerged through the fabric, it is inserted at the distance required for the length of the stitch.

Note: This stitch is usually formed with stranded silk or cotton to form centre details or stamens on flowers. The thread can be wrapped around the needle once, twice or more depending on the size of the knot required.

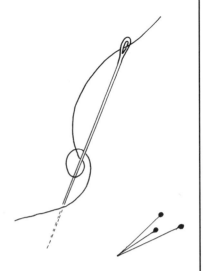

Feather Stitch

1   Bring the needle through the fabric at A, go down at B and emerge at C. The next stage of the stitch are these steps reversed to the other side.

2   The stitches are worked alternatively from one side to the other.

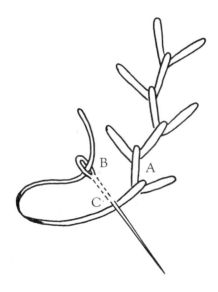

I use this stitch to form delicate foliage effects on some of the projects, usually in silver or gold thread, but occasionally in cotton or silk. It is also useful to fill in a space and balance a design without creating a bulky effect.

Formation of Flower Buds

Flower buds and partially opened flowers are formed using a combination of 3 stitches in both ribbon and stranded thread. The size of the bud formed is determined by the number of ribbon stitches worked together.

1 A single bud = 1 ribbon stitch + 1 fly stitch + 1 straight stitch.

2 A larger bud = 2 ribbon stitches + 1 fly stitch + 2 straight stitches.

3 A partially opened flower = 3 ribbon stitces + 1 fly stitch + 3 straight stitches.

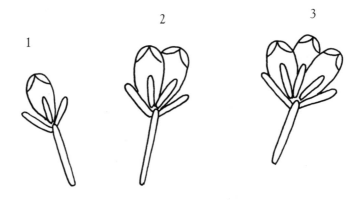

1 Single Bud = 1 ribbon stitch + 1 fly stitch + 1 straight stitch
2 Double Bud = 2 ribbon stitches + 1 fly stitch + 2 straight stitches
3 Partial Flowers = 3 ribbon stitches + 1 fly stitch + 3 straight stitches

Buds are formed using basic ribbon stitch in the desired colour. A fly stitch and a straight stitch are formed over this ribbon stitch as illustrated. An extra straight stitch is formed over each ribbon stitch included in the bud formation.

Both the straight stitch and the fly stitch are formed in stranded cotton to match whatever colour the stem or branch of the flower has been worked in.

If larger buds are required, the number of ribbon stitches is increased. Instead of details, such as a calyx around a bud, being added with thread, use silk ribbon in an appropriate width.

Formation of the Spider Web

Very early one morning I noticed on a clump of fern that grows in my garden, about 50 tiny perfect spider webs. The image of those webs stayed with me all day. That evening I was working on a garden landscape and decided to place a web, complete with a tiny spider, among the flowers. The tiny web has now become something of a trademark of my work and both students and friends look for it when they study a newly completed piece.

I use Madeira metallic sewing machine thread to create the webs, either in silver or gold. The spokes of the web are formed first — always an uneven number — in straight stitch. They are anchored to the flowers simply by stitching close to the leaf, bud, etc. The web is then formed by taking straight stitches, working from the outside to the centre between every alternate spoke in each round. It will take you two rounds of stitching between the spokes to complete one round of web. By working in this way, you will be able to put tension on the thread of the web as you create it and not pull the spokes unevenly by stitching over them.

Once you have completed this outside ring, move a little further in and complete a second round, third round, etc. It usually takes four to five rounds to complete the entire web.

The spider is simply formed by stitching a single wrap French knot using one strand of thread over one of the spokes.

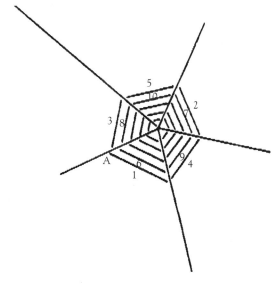

Painted Backgrounds

Painting backgrounds on which to embroider garden landscapes was my introduction to colouring fabric for embroidery. I still get immense enjoyment from creating simple landscape backgrounds, usually with a design feature, and then embroidering through the fabric to create the flowers that fill these gardens. Several of my garden landscapes feature as designs in this book.

I have also discovered that simple one-colour backgrounds increase the depth and visual interest of all embroidery work. More often than not, I now paint the fabric prior to embroidering the design, even though it may not be a design for a garden landscape. This step is optional for many of the designs in this book, but it does give you the opportunity to create a sense of perpective before you begin stitching. It works particularly well if your design incorporates flowers and shrubs which lend themselves to 'perspective stitching'.

Below are a number of helpful hints which you should keep in mind when painting fabric prior to starting your embroidery.

1   Pure silk, cotton, cotton velvet and wool are all suitable fabrics on which to paint a background, even though there are subtle differences between them. Most fabrics are worth trying.

2   Always work on dry, unwashed fabric.

3   Use acrylic folk art paint to create backgrounds. The wide range of colours available in the many brands on the market makes it easy to find the handful of colours required to prepare almost any background. I have a palette of four colours which I use most often — dark green, a lighter shade of green, light cream and a deeper caramel colour. For more complex designs, I occasionally add grey and light blue.

4   If you are working on an item which will require washing, for example a baby's blanket, a cushion or a bag, add an appropriate 'textile medium' to the paint prior to application. This will transform acrylic folk art paint into a fabric paint, ensuring that it will be colour fast and will not become 'crusty' on the fabric. Follow the manufacturer's directions, adding it to the paint in the correct ratio prior to diluting the paint. 'Set' the paint if required by the manufacturer.

5   Use an inexpensive bristle brush, or even a small sea sponge, to apply the paint. If painting on wool, a 'deersfoot' brush is recommended, as the paint needs to be stabbed into the pile of the fabric. This type of brush has short bristles which aid the application of the paint.

6   Water down the paint to the palest shade required before application. Paint can always be added to increase the depth of colour, but it is almost impossible to remove if applied too heavily. I would suggest a ratio of around 10–20 per cent paint and 90–80 per cent water. When this has been applied to the fabric, deeper highlights of the same colour can be added by applying a little more paint to areas where it is required.

7   Experiment with the shade on a scrap of the fabric you have chosen before applying the paint to the entire piece.

8   Completely dry an area of colour before introducing another colour. A hair dryer is a handy tool as it can be used to speed up the drying time, particularly between the application of different colours. It is also useful for quickly drying areas where too much water has been applied.

9   If you do happen to apply colour in one particular area in a deeper shade than you would have liked, don't try to remove it or water it down. Finish the painted backgound and then embroider over it. Chances are any small mistakes in the background can be covered with your ribbon embroidery and you will be the only one the wiser. You can also disguise any small areas where one colour has bled into another by strategically placing some suitable flowers over that section of your work.

Keep in mind that you are simply creating a background to embroider over. The painted background does not need to be the dominant feature, nor does it need to be too complicated. It will become an integral part of your work, but not the most important part. That should always be the hand embroidery.

Many of the projects featured have a pre-painted background. However, the decision to paint the background prior to embroidering is a personal one. I have included a list of the projects contained in this book and have noted beside each design whether the background is optional or a requirement for its success.

Introduction to the Projects

Many of the projects included in this book are useful everyday items which will give lasting pleasure. Some are special; some are designed to spoil you; some make lovely gifts for friends. I hope that all of them will appeal in some way.

In many instances, I have given alternatives to the designs featured or suggestions for other uses for them to broaden their appeal. The freedom to adapt or create your own designs and projects increases with experience.

At the end of each project, I have included a helpful hint which is relevant to that project and sometimes useful in other instances as well.

All the projects have been graded according to skill. The classifications are beginner, intermediate or advanced. These take into consideration the variety of embroidery stitches used in the project, the techniques and materials required, and whether a painted backgound is optional or essential. Mostly, there is little difference between an intermediate and beginner's project in the number of stitches used. The intermediate project just takes more time and effort to complete.

This grading system is simply a guide. If you are a beginner and would like to work an intermediate or advanced project, don't be afraid to do so.

The classifications, together with the painted background requirements for each project, appear in the 'Index to the Projects' on the following page.

Index to the Projects

Project	Painted Background	Skill Level	Page
Linen with Lavender	Not required	Beginner	31
Embroidered Lidded Boxes	Optional	Beginner	34
Antique Bolster Cushion	Not required	Beginner	39
Nanna's Knee Rug	Optional	Intermediate	45
Floral Tea Cosy	Optional	Intermediate	55
Lady's Lingerie Bag	Optional	Intermediate	61
Garden Lampshade	Optional	Intermediate	67
Blooming Baskets — A Garden Landscape	Required	Intermediate	74
Doiley Storage Sachet	Required	Advanced	81
Shhh! The Fairies Are Home — A Blanket	Required	Advanced	89

Linen with Lavender

You can welcome a special guest or simply spoil yourself with this embroidered linen set. A face towel, a generous bath towel and a cotton pillowcase have been embroidered with a delicate spray of lavender tied with a complementary silk bow. The spray of lavender has been embroidered on a scalloped-edge band of Aida cloth and can be lengthened if desired by adding longer stems to the flowers and more flower heads. The same design is embroidered on the band of each item.

REQUIREMENTS

Aida cotton band with scalloped edge, 50mm (2") wide x width of item.

Silk ribbons and stranded art silk as listed below.

Embroidery hoop.

Lavender Spray

Component	Thread	No.	Colour	Stitch Used
Stems	Rajmahal	926	Verdigris	Stem
Flower head	2mm silk	179	Medium grape	Ribbon
	2mm silk	23	Deep mauve	Ribbon
Leaves	4mm silk	74	Smoky grey-green	Ribbon
Bow	4mm silk	14	Pale yellow	Hand-tied bow

METHOD

1   Trim the Aida band to the length required to cover one edge of the linen plus 2.5cm (1"). This allows a little of the band to be turned under when it is sewn in place to neaten the cut edge.

NANNA'S KNEE RUG (DETAIL)

LINEN WITH LAVENDER

EMBROIDERED LIDDED BOXES AND LADY'S LINGERIE BAG

ANTIQUE BOLSTER CUSHION

2   Referring to the chart of stitches and threads above, work the embroidery. A tiny silver spider web has been added to the embroidery using 1 strand of silver Madeira metallic thread and straight stitches. The spider is a single wrap French knot using 2 strands of Rajmahal thread 29 (Charcoal).

3   Once the embroidery is complete and all ends have been fastened off, pin the embroidered band in place, with the ends turned under ready for stitching. When stitching the band to the pillowcase, make sure that you only stitch through one thickness of the pillowcase fabric. The ends can be neatened by hand or machine sewn. If required, the linen can be pressed after completion.

Handy Hint

The lavender flower heads are worked with two colours of silk ribbon. Don't attempt to work both colours at the same time; instead, work all the stitches in one colour and then add the stitches in the second colour. By working in this way, you avoid pulling any dangling threads or damaging completed stitches.

Embroidered Lidded Boxes

T his set of lidded boxes is a simple beginner's project as only three types of stitches have been used to create the flowers. Perspective stitching has been used to give them dimension and they have been placed on a pre-painted background to add further depth. Both hand-dyed ribbons (roses) and plain-dyed ribbons (daisies) have been incorporated in the design. Using different widths of the same colours has reduced the scale of the flowers in the design featured on the smaller box.

REQUIREMENTS

Satin-covered boxes (available from Rajmahal — see Stockists at end of book).

Fabric of your choice for embroidery (I used embossed satin).

Water erasable pen.

Decoart Americana folk art paint, DA52 (Avocado).

Bristle brush.

Silk ribbons and threads as detailed in the following flower guide (see Stockists).

Embroidery hoop.

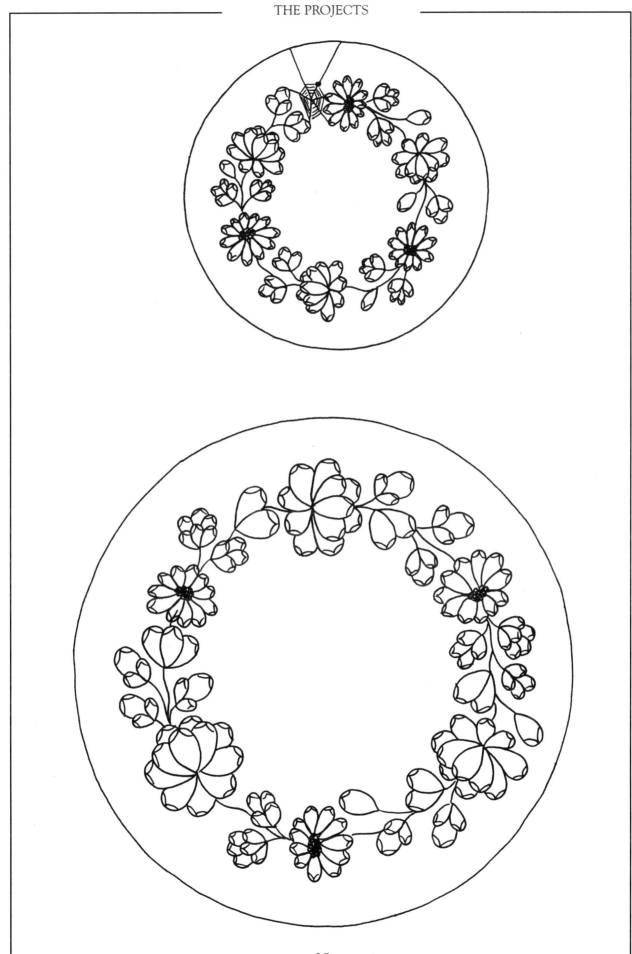

Large Lidded Box
Roses

Component	Thread	No.	Colour	Stitch Used
Roses	7mm silk		Petals Raspberry sorbet	Ribbon
Buds	7mm silk		Petals Raspberry sorbet	Ribbon
Calyx	4mm silk		Petals Rosemary	Ribbon
Leaves	7mm silk		Petals Rosemary	Ribbon
Stem	Rajmahal	421	Green earth	Stem

Daisies

Component	Thread	No.	Colour	Stitch Used
Flower centres	4mm silk	15	Bright yellow	French knots
Flower petals	4mm silk	1	Antique white	Ribbon
Buds	4mm silk	1	Antique white	Ribbon
Calyx	4mm silk	72	Dark jungle green	Ribbon
Stem	Rajmahal	421	Green earth	Stem

Small Lidded Box
Roses

Component	Thread	No.	Colour	Stitch Used
Roses	4mm silk		Petals Raspberry sorbet	Ribbon
Buds	4mm silk		Petals Raspberry sorbet	Ribbon
Calyx	4mm silk		Petals Rosemary	Ribbon
Leaves	4mm silk		Petals Rosemary	Ribbon
Stem	Rajmahal	421	Green earth	Stem

Daisies

Component	Thread	No.	Colour	Stitch Used
Flower centres	2mm silk	15	Bright yellow	French knots
Flower petals	1mm silk	1	Antique white	Ribbon
Buds	1mm silk	1	Antique white	Ribbon
Calyx	4mm silk	72	Dark jungle green	Ribbon
Stem	Rajmahal	421	Green earth	Stem

Please note: Not all colours are available in each different width ribbon so 4mm ribbon has been used to form the calyxes for the flowers in both designs. The scale will still be reduced by working the full flowers in the narrower ribbon.

METHOD

1   Remove the top from the lidded box and place in the centre of your fabric. Use a water erasable pen to trace around this, marking the external boundary of the design. Using the design sheet, draw a line to indicate the position of the garland of flowers.

2   Prepare the painted backgrounds by applying the paint to the fabric within the boundary marked (see section on 'Painted Backgrounds'). Allow to dry completely.

3   Once again using the design sheet, mark the full flowers and the buds on the background and work them according to the thread and stitch guide above. When complete, use the ribbons to complete the leaves and the calyx for each bud. Finally, work the stems.

4   If required, add the spider web and spider. The tiny silver spider web has been embroidered using 1 strand of silver Madeira metallic thread and straight stitches. The spider is a single wrap French knot using 2 strands of Rajmahal thread 29 (Charcoal).

5   Remove any visible marks from the marking pen using a cotton bud dipped in cold water.

6   Using a double strand of strong cotton thread, work a row of neat tacking stitches around the edge of the work, 12mm (½") from the outside boundary. Place the embroidery face down on a clean surface and put the

disc from the lidded box face down and centred on the embroidery. Use the tails of the thread to gently, but firmly, draw in the tacking stitches until the fabric is drawn tightly over the disc. Tie off the threads in a double knot. Adjust the gathers if necessary.

7   Glue the disc onto the top of the lid.

HANDY HINT

If a design is too small or too large for the area that you intend to cover with embroidery, scale the flower size using different width ribbons as on these boxes. Lengthening petals tends to distort the appearance of a flower. Using a narrower or wider ribbon, depending on the size variation required, is much more effective.

Antique
Bolster Cushion

The embossed pure silk fabric and hand-dyed ribbon colours used for this project were carefully chosen to evoke memories of times past. This bolster cushion features a climbing rose worked in only two colours of overdyed ribbon. The subtle shades of the silk ribbons and the richness of the fabric create dimension in the embroidery, while the two lace butterflies enhance its antique quality. The cushion is finished with a piping cord on each side of the embroidered panel and at the opposite end of the cushion. The ends of the cushion are drawn in with two cords hand-made from Rajmahal thread.

REQUIREMENTS

Fabric for cushion, 58cm wide x 64cm long (23" x 25").

Piping cord.

Fusible interfacing, such as Armorweft.

Water erasable pen.

Ribbons and threads as detailed below.

Embroidery hoop.

Two lace butterfly motifs.

Bolster-style cushion insert, 17cm x 40cm (7" x 16").

POSITION OF PIPING CORD

LEFT HAND
SIDE

POSITION OF PIPING CORD

MIDDLE

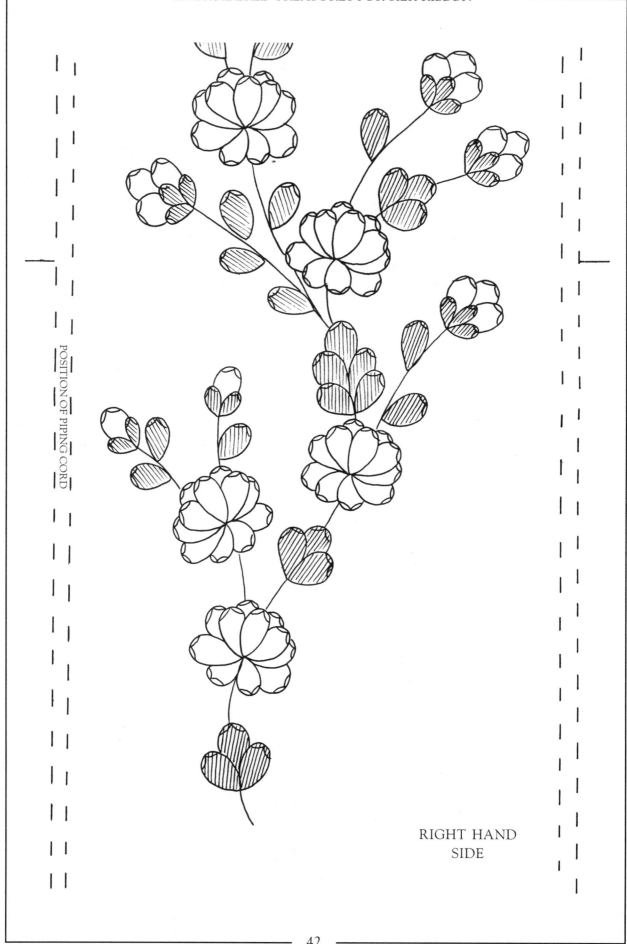

POSITION OF PIPING CORD

RIGHT HAND
SIDE

Climbing Rose

Component	Thread	No.	Colour	Stitch Used
Stems	Rajmahal	421	Green earth	Stem stitch, 2 strands
Full blown rose	7mm silk		Petals Brown sugar	Ribbon
Buds	7mm silk		Petals Brown sugar	Ribbon
Bud calyx	4mm silk		Petals Oregano	Ribbon
Leaves	4mm silk		Petals Oregano	Ribbon

METHOD

1   Press the fabric along the lines where the piping is to be placed if you wish to incorporate this in the finished piece. Place the piping cord inside the fabric. Make sure that it butts up to the fold and, using the zipper foot on your machine, stitch as close as possible to the cord. Repeat for the other two piping cords.

2   Press a strip of iron-on interfacing on the wrong side of the fabric between the piping cords which outline the embroidered panel.

3   Using a water erasable pen, mark the delicate curving lines which form the stems of the rose. Work these in stem stitch using 2 strands of Rajmahal thread.

4   Following the design illustration, work the full blown roses as above. Generally, these are placed where the stems branch. Work the buds at the ends of the stems. The calyx detail is worked once all the buds have been completed, 2 or 3 stitches forming each calyx. (These stitches are shaded on the diagram.) Work the leaves last, in groups, as shown.

5   Finally, work the spider web and spider if required. The tiny silver spider web has been embroidered using 1 strand of silver Madeira metallic thread and straight stitches. The spider is a single wrap French knot using 2 strands of Rajmahal thread 29 (Charcoal).

6   Stitch the butterfly motifs in place using matching thread.

7   Once the embroidery is complete, stitch the centre back 1.5cm (¾") seam, matching the rows of piping. Press

this seam open. Fold over a 6mm allowance at each end and then fold over again 1.5cm (¾"). Stitch this fold along the edge to form the cord casing at each end of the cushion.

8　Thread 2 twisted cords of Rajmahal thread 171 (Woodlands) through the casing.

9　Place the bolster cushion insert inside the cushion cover. Gently draw the cords in and tie in a loose bow. A scrap of the fabric can be placed inside the end of the cushion to hide the cushion insert.

HANDY HINT

When choosing your fabric, consider the colour and texture carefully as different fabrics create very different effects. The same cushion and embroidery design worked on a pale-coloured fabric with pastel-toned ribbons would result in an entirely different appearance.

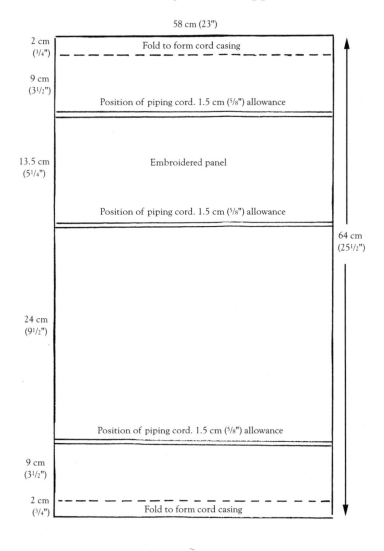

58 cm (23")

2 cm (¾") — Fold to form cord casing

9 cm (3½") — Position of piping cord. 1.5 cm (⅝") allowance

13.5 cm (5¼") — Embroidered panel — Position of piping cord. 1.5 cm (⅝") allowance

24 cm (9½") — Position of piping cord. 1.5 cm (⅝") allowance

64 cm (25½")

9 cm (3½")

2 cm (¾") — Fold to form cord casing

Nanna's
Knee Rug

This pure wool blanket featuring a traditional cottage garden has been lined with a complementary cotton fabric and edged with delicate guipure lace to create additional interest. The hand-painted background to the flowers, which is optional, has been created using one colour only, but it does give a greater depth to the embroidery.

REQUIREMENTS

Wool blanketing, cot or knee rug size, approximately 76cm x 114cm (30" x 45").

Water erasable fabric marking pen.

Folk art paint.

Textile medium.

Deersfoot or bristle brush.

Tulle.

Permanent black marking pen.

Klipfast frame or quilting hoop.

Ribbons and threads as listed below.

Embroidery hoop.

Cotton fabric to line the blanket, approximately 15cm (6") wider and longer than the piece of blanketing to allow for the turned edges.

Guipure lace.

Satin-edged ribbon for the corner bows if required.

The flowers are listed as they appear on the rug (from left to right).

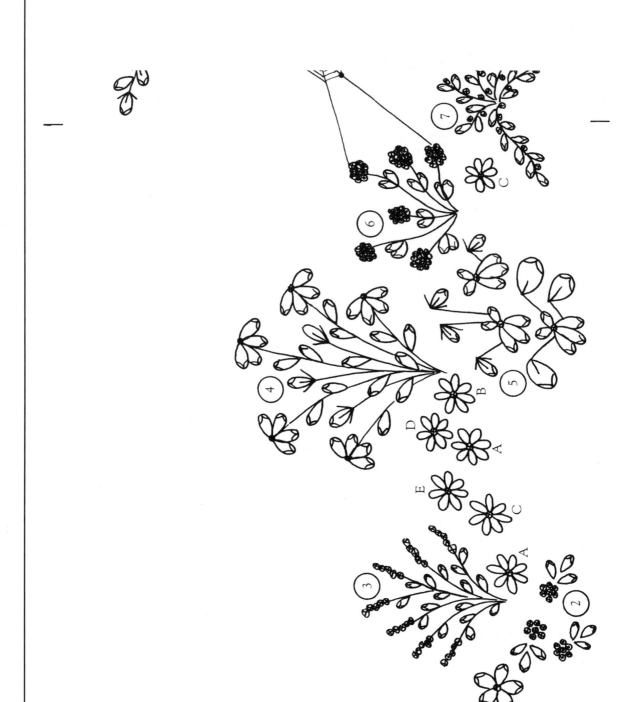

LEFT HAND
SIDE

MIDDLE

RIGHT HAND
SIDE

NANNA'S KNEE RUG

FLORAL TEA COSY

GARDEN LAMPSHADE

BLOOMING BASKETS — A GARDEN LANDSCAPE

1 Pink Daisies

Component	Thread	No.	Colour	Stitch Used
Petals	4mm silk	5	Very pale pink	Ribbon
Centres	4mm silk	114	Deep rose pink	French knots
Leaves	4mm silk	31	Light apple green	Ribbon

2 Blue Forget-me-nots

Component	Thread	No.	Colour	Stitch Used
Petals	4mm silk	125	Light blue	French knots
Centres	4mm silk	15	Bright yellow	French knots
Leaves	2mm silk	31	Light apple green	Ribbon

3 Blue Salvia

Component	Thread	No.	Colour	Stitch Used
Stem	Rajmahal	521	Maidenhair	Stem
Leaves	2mm silk	20	Medium grass green	Ribbon
Flowers	4mm silk	118	Deep blue-mauve	French knots

4 White Daisies

Component	Thread	No	Colour	Stitch Used
Stems	Rajmahal	521	Maidenhair	Stem
Petals	4mm silk	3	White	Ribbon
Centres	4mm silk	15	Bright yellow	French knots
Leaves	4mm silk	20	Medium grass green	Ribbon

5 Violets

Component	Thread	No.	Colour	Stitch Used
Centres	4mm silk	15	Bright yellow	French knots
Petals/buds	4mm silk	85	Deep purple	Ribbon
Stems	Rajmahal	521	Maidenhair	Fly/straight
Leaves	7mm silk	20	Medium grass green	Ribbon

6 Geranium

Component	Thread	No.	Colour	Stitch Used
Stem	Rajmahal	65	Laurel green	Stem
Flowers	4mm silk	114	Deep rose pink	French knots
Leaves	4mm silk	72	Dark jungle green	Ribbon

7 Erigeron

Component	Thread	No.	Colour	Stitch Used
Stem	Rajmahal	926	Verdigris	Stem
Leaves	2mm silk	33	Medium blue-green	Ribbon
Flowers	4mm silk	3	White	French knots

8 Blue Hyacinths

Component	Thread	No.	Colour	Stitch Used
Stem	Rajmahal	521	Maidenhair	Stem
Leaves	4mm silk	72	Dark jungle green	Ribbon
Flowers	4mm silk	44	Medium sky blue	French knots

9 Standard Rose Bush

Component	Thread	No.	Colour	Stitch Used
Stem	Rajmahal	521	Maidenhair	Stem stitch (2 rows)
Branches	Rajmahal	521	Maidenhair	Stem
Leaves	4mm silk	20	Medium grass green	Ribbon
Flowers	4mm silk	122	Light candy pink	Spider web/woven rose
Buds	4mm silk	122	Light candy pink	Ribbon
Bud details	Rajmahal	521	Maidenhair	Fly/straight

10 Lavender

Component	Thread	No.	Colour	Stitch Used
Stem	Rajmahal	926	Verdigris	Stem
Leaves	2mm silk	32	Light blue-green	Ribbon
Flowers	2mm silk	23	Deep mauve	French knots
	2mm silk	179	Medium grape	French knots

11 Pink Forget-me-nots

Component	Thread	No.	Colour	Stitch Used
Centres	4mm silk	15	Bright yellow	French knot
Petals	4mm silk	163	Very light rose pink	French knots
Leaves	2mm silk	31	Light apple green	Ribbon

12 Lily-of-the-Valley

Component	Thread	No.	Colour	Stitch Used
Stem	Rajmahal	65	Laurel green	Stem
Leaves	2mm silk	21	Dark forest green	Ribbon
Flowers	4mm silk	3	White	French knots

13 Foxgloves

Component	Thread	No.	Colour	Stitch Used
Stem	Rajmahal	926	Verdigris	Stem
Flowers	4mm silk	46	Deep blue	Ribbon
	4mm silk	44	Medium sky blue	stitch and
	4mm silk	125	Light blue	French
	4mm silk	90	Very pale sky blue	knots
Leaves	4mm silk	33	Medium blue-green	Ribbon

14 Violets

As for those detailed in 5.

15 Yellow Daisies

Component	Thread	No.	Colour	Stitch Used
Stem	Rajmahal	521	Maidenhair	Stem
Centres	4mm silk	15	Bright yellow	French knot
Petals/buds	4mm silk	14	Pale yellow	Ribbon
Leaves	4mm silk	20	Medium grass green	Ribbon

16 Blue Forget-me-nots

As for those detailed in 2.

17 Grape Hyacinths

Component	Thread	No.	Colour	Stitch Used
Stem	Rajmahal	521	Maidenhair	Stem
Leaves	4mm silk	72	Dark jungle green	Extended ribbon stitch
Flowers	4mm silk	117	Light blue-mauve	French knots

18 Pink Daisies

As for those detailed in 1.

Anemones and Ranunculus

The anemones and ranunculus used as groundcover flowers at the base of the flower garden are worked in ribbon stitch in 2mm ribbon with a French knot centre of Rajmahal thread 29 (Charcoal). For positions, please refer to the letters on the diagram. The colours for the flower petals are as follows.

Component	Thread	No.	Colour
A	2mm silk	127	Light raspberry pink
B	2mm silk	15	Bright yellow
C	2mm silk	13	Lemon
D	2mm silk	179	Deep mauve
E	2mm silk	179	Medium grape

METHOD

1   If a painted background is required, do this before transferring the embroidery design to the blanket. Mark the centre of the blanket with a pin. Mark the boundaries of the embroidery on the blanket surface with the water erasable pen. This need only be a simple line, following the outline of the design, to which you work with the paint.

2   Blend the paint and the textile medium together to create the required shade of green. Water down a small amount of paint on a plate to create a colour wash. Using a deersfoot or bristle brush, apply the paint using a stabbing technique to penetrate the blanket pile. Pure wool blanketing is naturally resistant to water so you will have to stab the brush quite hard so that the paint actually reaches the woven threads of the blanketing through the fluffy pile. Vary the amount of colour wash you apply in different areas, darker beneath the centre

flower groups and lighter towards the edges. Keep refer-ring to the embroidery design to determine the areas which need an application of colour.

3   Transfer the embroidery design using one of two methods. Either hand draw the simple lines or dots required to denote the stems or flower centres with a water erasable pen by copying from the diagram (this is the method I use), or lay tulle over the diagram and use a permanent marking pen to mark the centres of the flowers and stems onto the tulle. Allow the pen marks to dry. Then place the tulle overlay into position over the painted background area and, once again using the water erasable pen, trace through the tulle over the black pen outlines to transfer the design. Remove the tulle. You will now have an indication of the position of the flowers and stems. Because of the pile of the blanketing, these lines will be faint so you may have to go over them again without the tulle.

4   Fit the piece of blanketing into either a Klipfast frame or a loosely tensioned quilting hoop. Although the blanketing is bulky in the frame, I have found that it is easier to work in this way because it keeps the area you are working on flat and does not bruise the blanketing as an embroidery hoop would do. (A large quilting hoop would also work well for this project as it can be adjusted to allow the blanketing to fit.) Always remember to remove the work from the frame when you are not working on it as this will minimise the marks left by the frame.

5   The silk ribbons and threads used to create the flower groups are listed, along with the stitches used, from the left to the right of the design. I began stitching in the centre of the design, at the standard rose, and worked to the left. I then moved to the right side of the design. Remember to keep the tension quite loose when using silk ribbon so that the stitches sit up 'proud' of the blanketing. If the stitches are pulled as they are formed, they will be buried in the pile and the soft effect of the silk on the wool will be lost. Wool blanketing is a very soft fabric which works well with silk, minimising the 'distressing' that can occur when you work on other fabrics. After the stitching is complete, use a cotton bud dipped in cold water to remove any water erasable pen marks still visible.

6   The tiny spider web has once again been added to the flowers. It has been created using 1 strand of silver Madeira machine sewing thread. Straight stitches were used for the spokes and a succession of straight stitches for the actual web. The tiny spider was formed from a single wrap French knot using 1 strand of Rajmahal thread 29 (Charcoal).

7   The blanket is lined with the pure cotton fabric which is 15cm (6") larger than the blanket piece to allow for a generous turn-under and a border of 5cm (2") around the entire blanket. The corners of this fabric are mitred and the lining is hand-stitched in place using a fine hem stitch.

8   For additional decoration, hand-stitch guipure lace to the edge of the lining fabric and stitch a simple bow made from satin-edged ribbon to each corner.

HANDY HINT

A neater finish will be achieved by hand-stitching the lining fabric to the blanket. If a sewing machine is used, it may cause the different weights of fabric to pucker, making them difficult to sew together. In addition, an unsightly row of stitching will be visible on the reverse of the blanket.

Floral Tea Cosy

T his pretty item is suitable for everyday use in the family home. It has been worked on pure wool blanketing in a superb plum colour and the painted background, which is optional, has been created using only two shades of green, light and dark. The wool blanketing is very easy to work on, making this design suitable for a beginner who would like to attempt both a painted background and flowers which lend themselves to perspective stitching. The tea cosy is fully lined with a complementary cotton fabric which is hand-stitched in place. Assembling this work involves straight stitching only. A simple drawstring closes the top of the tea cosy.

REQUIREMENTS

2 pieces of pure wool blanketing or wool fabric, 30cm x 22cm (12" x 8¾").

Water erasable marking pen.

Ribbons and threads as listed below.

Embroidery hoop.

Cotton fabric for lining, 35cm x 22cm (14" x 8½").

Additional lining fabric for cord casing and drawstring.

The flowers are listed as they appear on the design (from left to right).

1 Salvia

Component	Thread	No.	Colour	Stitch Used
Stems	Rajmahal	521	Maidenhair	Stem
Flowers	4mm silk	117	Light blue-mauve	French knots
Leaves	2mm silk	20	Medium grass green	Ribbon

2 White Dianthus

Component	Thread	No.	Colour	Stitch Used
Stems	Rajmahal	521	Maidenhair	Stem
Leaves	2mm silk	21	Dark forest green	Extended ribbon stitch
Flowers	2mm silk	3	White	French knots

3 Pink Daisies

Component	Thread	No.	Colour	Stitch Used
Stems	Rajmahal	521	Maidenhair	Stem
Flower centres	4mm silk	15	Bright yellow	French knots
Petals	4mm silk	5	Very pale pink	Ribbon
Buds	4mm silk	5	Very pale pink	Ribbon
Bud details	Rajmahal	521	Maidenhair	Fly/straight
Leaves	4mm silk	72	Dark jungle green	Ribbon

4 Primula

Component	Thread	No.	Colour	Stitch Used
Stems	Rajmahal	521	Maidenhair	Stem/straight
Flowers	4mm silk	128	Raspberry pink	French knots
Leaves	4mm silk	21	Dark forest green	Ribbon

5 Hydrangeas

Component	Thread	No.	Colour	Stitch Used
Stems	Rajmahal	521	Maidenhair	Stem
Flowers	4mm silk		Colour Streams Wisteria	French knots
Leaves	7mm silk	20	Medium grass green	Ribbon

6 Freesias

Component	Thread	No.	Colour	Stitch Used
Stems	Rajmahal	521	Maidenhair	Stem
Leaves	2mm silk	20	Medium grass green	Extended ribbon stitch
Flowers	2mm silk	13	Pale lemon	Ribbon stitch and French knots

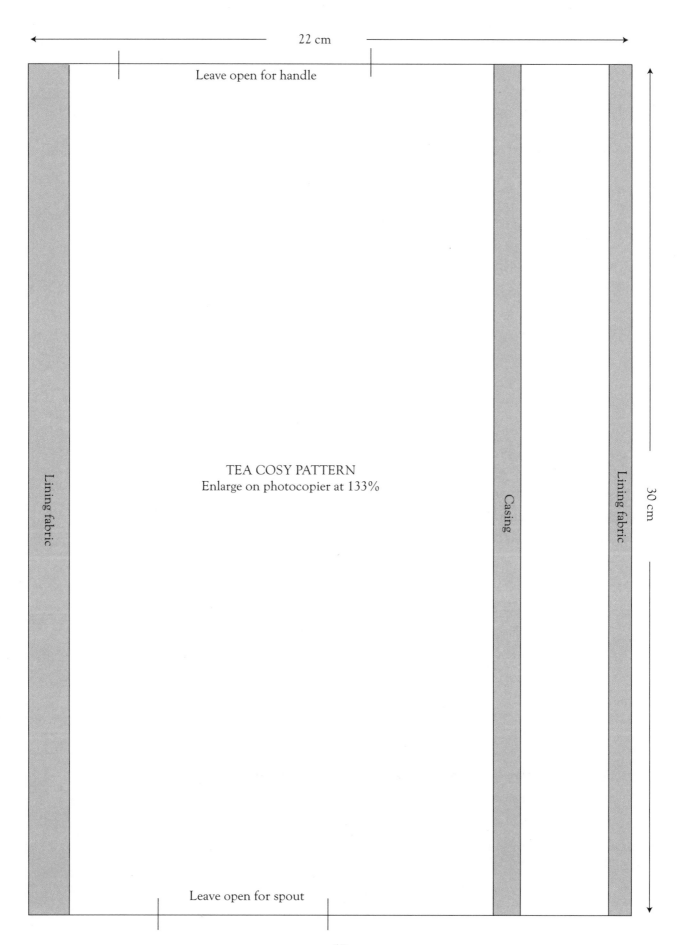

22 cm

Leave open for handle

Lining fabric

Casing

Lining fabric

30 cm

TEA COSY PATTERN
Enlarge on photocopier at 133%

Leave open for spout

7 Anemones and Ranunculus

Scattered at the base of the flowers are single flowers designed to fill in the remaining spaces and to balance the colours. They are all worked in ribbon stitch using 2mm silk in the following colours: 13 (Pale lemon), 179 (Medium grape), 128 (Raspberry pink), 65 (Light caramel, 23 (Deep mauve). All have a French knot centre in 4mm black silk ribbon. The leaves have been worked in 2mm silk, 33 (Medium blue-green).

Method

1   Using the pattern sheet as a guide, mark in the major stem lines and the centres of the flowers which form the groundcover with a water erasable marking pen (see 'Materials and Techniques'). This will give you an indication of where you need to apply the painted background wash.

2   Water a tiny drop of each paint colour down until they are the desired colours and consistencies and, using a stabbing motion, apply to the wool following the markings. Allow to dry completely. Once the paint is dry, you can commence the embroidery.

3   When the embroidery has been completed, add the spider web and spider if required. The tiny silver spider web is embroidered using 1 strand of silver Madeira metallic thread and straight stitches only. The spider is a single wrap French knot worked with 2 strands of Rajmahal thread 29 (Charcoal).

4   The tea cosy can now be assembled. Cut the lining fabric to the same width as the wool fabric but 5 cm (2") longer to allow for the top and bottom seam allowance and the decorative folded edge. Mark both the wool fabric and the lining fabric with the correct positions for the teapot handle and spout. Using a 6mm (¼") seam allowance, stitch the wool fabric together at the side seams leaving open spaces between the marks. Repeat for the lining fabric. Press the seams open.

5   Cut a strip of lining fabric 2.5cm (1") wide to form the casing. Fold and press the edges to neaten. Sew the strip of fabric to the outside of the wool fabric 4.5cm (1¾") from the top edge, leaving an opening at the centre back of the tea cosy to allow the cord to be threaded through.

6   Cut a second strip of fabric the same width and fold the edges and press. Fold this in half once again and sew along the edge to create a drawstring.

7   Place the lining inside the tea cosy with the wrong sides of the fabric together. Pin in place. Hand sew the lining to the wool at both the spout and handle openings. Turn over the top and bottom of the lining fabric to the right side of the tea cosy and evenly stitch this fabric in place.

8   Thread the cord through the casing and draw the top of the tea cosy closed. Tie a bow and decorate the ends of the cord with decorative beads if desired.

HANDY HINT

A sewing tool known as a 'bias maker' is useful for making the casing and the cord. Since these strips of fabric do not need to be sewn around a curve or circle, it is not necessary to cut them 'on the bias'. They can be cut on the straight grain of the fabric. However, the bias maker allows the simultaneous turning and pressing of the edges, giving a very neat and even finish.

Lady's
Lingerie Bag

❧✦❧

Worked on pure silk fabric, this lovely lingerie bag features a garden landscape of traditional flowers on a subtle hand-painted background. The painted background, which is optional, has been created using one colour only. The design is also suitable for framing, or for decorating other items, such as a hot water-bottle cover. This lingerie sachet has been fully lined with a fine lining fabric and has a guipure lace trim. A twisted cord made from Rajmahal stranded art silk finishes the project.

REQUIREMENTS

Dupion silk, 50cm x 60cm (20" x 24").

Iron-on flexible interfacing, 50cm x 60cm (20" x 24").

Decoart Americana folk art paint, DA52 (Avocado).

Embroidery hoop.

Silk embroidery ribbons and threads as detailed in the following guide to the flowers.

Lining fabric, 50cm x 60cm (20" x 24").

Guipure lace edging, 60cm (24") length.

2 skeins of Rajmahal thread for twisted cord (colour to complement project fabric).

2 decorative beads.

The flowers are listed as they appear on the design (from left to right).

1 Groundcover Daisies

Component	Thread	No.	Colour	Stitch Used
Centres	4mm silk	15	Bright yellow	French knot
Petals	4mm silk	13	Pale lemon	Ribbon

2 Anemones

Component	Thread	No.	Colour	Stitch Used
Stems	Rajmahal	805	Sassafras	Stem
Centres	Rajmahal	29	Charcoal	2 wrap French knot
Petals	2mm silk	179	Medium grape	Ribbon
	2mm silk	22	Light mauve	Ribbon
Buds	2mm silk	114	Deep rose pink	Ribbon
Bud detail	Rajmahal	805	Sassafras	Fly/straight
Leaves	2mm silk	33	Medium blue-green	Ribbon

3 Hybrid Tea Rose Bush

Component	Thread	No.	Colour	Stitch Used
Stems	Rajmahal	521	Maidenhair	Stem
Roses	4mm silk	157	Very light dusky pink	Spider web/ woven rose
Buds	4mm silk	157	Very light dusky pink	Ribbon
Leaves	4mm silk	72	Dark jungle green	Ribbon
Bud details	Rajmahal	521	Maidenhair	Fly/straight

4 Forget-me-nots

Component	Thread	No.	Colour	Stitch Used
Centres	4mm silk	15	Bright yellow	French knot
Petals	4mm silk	125	Light blue	French knots
Leaves	4mm silk	31	Light apple green	Ribbon

5 Viola Tricolour

Component	Thread	No.	Colour	Stitch Used
Centres	4mm silk	15	Bright yellow	French knot
Upper petals	4mm silk	84	Purple	Ribbon
Lower petals	4mm silk	156	Dark cream	Ribbon
Lower petals	4mm silk	13	Pale lemon	Ribbon
Flower details	Rajmahal	29	Charcoal	Straight
Buds	4mm silk	84	Purple	Ribbon
Bud details	Rajmahal	521	Maidenhair	Fly/straight

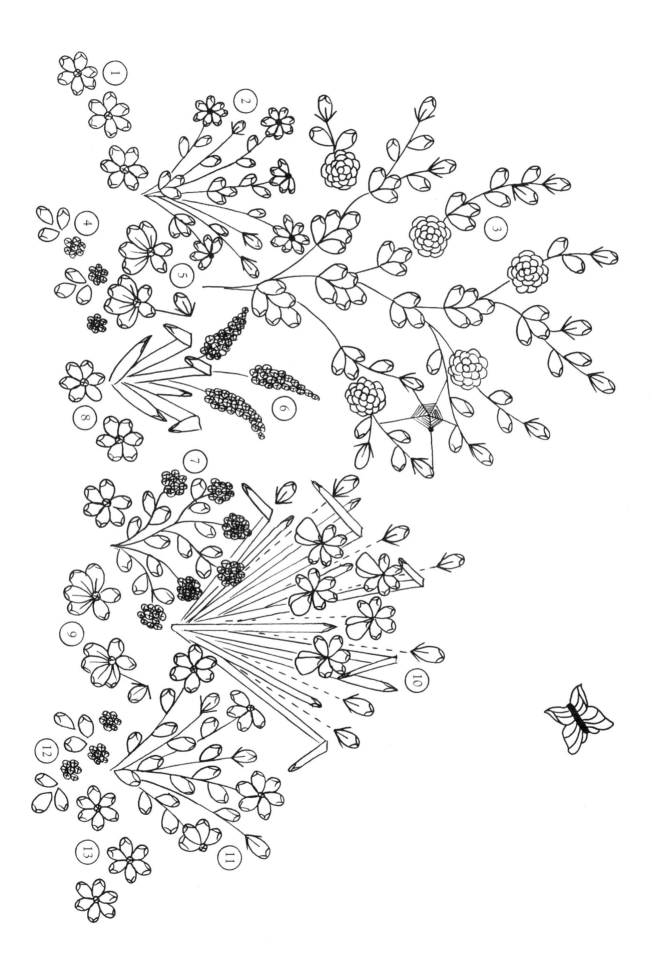

6 Grape Hyacinths

Component	Thread	No.	Colour	Stitch Used
Stems	Rajmahal	65	Laurel green	Stem
Flowers	4mm silk	102	Deep mauve	French knots
Leaves	4mm	21	Dark forest green	Extended/couched ribbon stitch

7 Geranium

Component	Thread	No.	Colour	Stitch Used
Stems	Rajmahal	521	Maidenhair	Stem
Flowers	4mm silk	112	Light rose pink	French knots
Leaves	4mm silk	171	Medium olive green	Ribbon

8 Lemon Groundcover Daisies

As for those detailed in 1.

9 Viola Tricolour

As for those detailed in 5.

10 Daffodils

Component	Thread	No.	Colour	Stitch Used
Leaves	2mm silk	33	Medium blue-green	Extended/couched ribbon stitch
Trumpet	4mm silk	15	Bright yellow	Loop
Petals	2mm silk	13	Pale lemon	Ribbon
Buds	4mm silk	15	Bright yellow	Ribbon
Stems/details	Rajmahal	805	Sassafras	Fly/straight stitch

11 Daisies

Component	Thread	No.	Colour	Stitch Used
Stems	Rajmahal	521	Maidenhair	Stem
Centres	4mm silk	15	Bright yellow	French knot
Petals/buds	4mm silk	1	Antique white	Ribbon
Bud detail	Rajmahal	521	Maidenhair	Fly/straight
Leaves	4mm silk	20	Medium grass green	Ribbon

12 Forget-me-nots

As for those detailed in 4.

13 Lemon Groundcover Daisies

As for those detailed in 1.

METHOD

1   Cut two rectangles from the silk fabric, 50cm x 30cm (20" x 12"). Iron the interfacing to the fabric. Overlock or zig-zag around the edges to prevent fraying.

2   Using the pattern sheet as a guide and your preferred method of design transfer (see 'Materials and Techniques'), mark the major stem lines and the centres of the flowers which form the groundcover onto your fabric. This will give you an indication of where you need to apply the painted background wash. Water down a tiny drop of paint until it is the desired colour and consistency and, using a stabbing motion, apply to the silk following the stem lines, etc. Apply the paint sparingly as additional depth of colour can always be achieved. Allow to dry completely.

3   Once the paint is dry, fit the fabric into a hoop large enough to encompass the entire design area and commence the embroidery following the guide above. When complete, use a cotton bud dipped in cold water to remove any visible marks from the marking pen.

4   The spider web and spider can be added at this stage. The spider web has been embroidered using 1 strand of silver Madeira metallic thread and straight stitches only. The spider is a single wrap French knot from 2 strands of Rajmahal thread 29 (Charcoal).

5   The bag and lining are made up separately and then joined at the top to form a casing for the twisted cord. With right sides together, sew up the side and bottom seams of the silk rectangles. Turn right side out. Press the edges of the bag. Fold in 7cm (2¾") at the top of the bag and press this fold flat. Make up the lining in the same manner from two rectangles of the lining fabric, 50cm x 30cm (20" x 12"), but fold out 7cm (2¾") at the top of the bag. Press fold flat. Stitch the lace on the folded edge of the lining. Insert the lining inside the silk with wrong sides together. Pin in place. Machine stitch approximately 5cm (2") and 6cm (2½") from the folded edges through both bags. This will form the cord casing and hide all seams. Unpick the side seam stitching on the silk bag only for 1cm (½") between the stitching lines which form the casing. This will allow you to thread the hand-made twisted cord. The cord is threaded through from both sides so that the top of the bag will close evenly. The decorative beads are added to the ends of the cord.

6 A tiny metal butterfly charm has been stitched above the garden to add further interest.

HANDY HINT

By threading two cords through a casing line, one from each side, you ensure that a bag draws closed evenly. Decorative beads used to cover knots in a cord can be held permanently in place by using a little glue inside the bead.

Garden
Lampshade

A simple garden of cottage flowers decorates the Oznaburg fabric used to make this country-style lampshade. The garden features a hand-painted one-colour background which adds interest to this simple garden project. The lampshade is lined with a cotton homespun fabric. The design is readily adaptable to different-shaped or sized lampshades.

REQUIREMENTS

Oznaburg cotton homespun fabric, approximately 50cm (20") length. (If you are adapting the design to suit a larger or different-shaped shade, more fabric may be required.)

Fabric marking pen.

Decoart Americana folk art paint, DA52 (Avocado).

Decoart textile medium.

Silk ribbons and threads as listed below.

Embroidery hoop.

Wire lampshade form.

Cotton tape to wind around the top and bottom of the lampshade.

Lining fabric, approximately 50cm (20") length.

Elastic.

1 Freesias

Component	Thread	No.	Colour	Stitch Used
Stems	Rajmahal	521	Maidenhair	Stem
Flowers	2mm silk	13	Pale lemon	French knots and ribbon stitch
Leaves	2mm silk	20	Medium grass green	Extended ribbon stitch

2 Grape Hyacinth

Component	Thread	No.	Colour	Stitch Used
Stems	Rajmahal	521	Maidenhair	Stem
Flowers	4mm silk	23	Deep mauve	French knots
Leaves	4mm silk	20	Medium grass green	Extended/couched ribbon stitch

3 Daffodils

Component	Thread	No.	Colour	Stitch Used
Leaves	2mm silk	32	Light blue-green	Extended/couched ribbon stitch
Flower trumpet	4mm silk	15	Bright yellow	Loop
Petals	2mm silk	13	Pale lemon	Ribbon
Flower buds	4mm silk	15	Bright Yellow	Ribbon
Details/stems	Rajmahal	805	Sassafras	Fly/straight stitch

4 Rose Bush

Component	Thread	No.	Colour	Stitch Used
Stems	Rajmahal	521	Maidenhair	Stem
Roses	4mm silk	105	Very pale orange	Spider web/woven rose
Buds	4mm silk	105	Very pale orange	Ribbon
Leaves	4mm silk	72	Dark jungle green	Ribbon
Bud details	Rajmahal	521	Maidenhair	Fly/straight

5 Dutch Hyacinths

Component	Thread	No.	Colour	Stitch Used
Stems	Rajmahal	521	Maidenhair	Stem
Flowers	4mm silk	14	Pale yellow	French knots
Leaves	4mm silk	20	Medium grass green	Extended/ couched ribbon stitch

6 Lavender

Component	Thread	No.	Colour	Stitch Used
Stems	Rajmahal	805	Sassafras	Stem
Flowers	4mm silk	178	Light grape	French knots
Leaves	4mm silk	33	Medium blue-green	Ribbon

7 Foxgloves

Component	Thread	No.	Colour	Stitch Used
Stems	Rajmahal	805	Sassafras	Stem
Flowers	4mm silk	44	Medium sky blue	French knots and ribbon stitch
	4mm silk	125	Light blue	
	4mm silk	90	Very pale sky blue	
Leaves	4mm silk	32	Light blue-green	Extended ribbon stitch

8 Yellow Daisies

Component	Thread	No.	Colour	Stitch Used
Stems	Rajmahal	521	Maidenhair	Stem
Flower centres	4mm silk	15	Bright yellow	French knots
Petals	4mm silk	13	Pale lemon	Ribbon
Leaves	2mm silk	20	Medium grass green	Ribbon

9 Viola Tricolour

Component	Thread	No.	Colour	Stitch Used
Flower centres	4mm silk	15	Bright yellow	French knots
Petals (upper)	4mm silk	85	Deep purple	Ribbon
Petals (lower)	4mm silk	13	Pale lemon	Ribbon
Petals (lower)	4mm silk	156	Dark cream	Ribbon
Flower details	Rajmahal	29	Charcoal	Straight

10 Groundcover Daisies

Component	Thread	No.	Colour	Stitch Used
Flower centres	4mm silk	15	Bright yellow	French knots
Petals	4mm silk	156	Dark cream	Ribbon
Leaves	4mm silk	72	Dark jungle green	Ribbon

METHOD

1   Place the design sheet 10cm (4") from the lower edge of the fabric. Using a fabric marking pen, mark the major stem lines and the position of the groundcover flowers. This will give you an indication of the painted background area. Mix the folk art paint and the textile medium to the consistency recommended by the manufacturer and water down well. Add the painted highlights to the fabric where the cottage garden flowers will be worked. Allow to dry and set as recommended by the manufacturer.

2   Once again use the marking pen and the design sheet to mark in the stem lines and the centres of the groundcover flowers. Using the threads and ribbons as detailed, work the flowers in the order in which they are listed. By working the flowers in this order, some flowers can overlap others, giving a further dimension to your work. Remove any visible marks made by the marking pen by using a cotton bud dipped in cold water.

3   Bind the bottom and top of the lampshade with cotton edge tape. This will give you something to which to stitch the edges of the shade when completed.

4 Stitch a centre back seam in the embroidered fabric to make it just large enough to fit over the wire shape. Machine stitch the lining fabric to make a similar cylinder. Press the seams open. Place the wrong sides of both fabrics together and trim the bottom edge so that the embroidery is approximately 2cm (¾") from this edge. Using a bias tape maker, make a length of tape to bind the two edges together. Stitch this tape in place, fold over and hand-stitch the other folded edge in place.

5 Slip the shade over the wire frame and determine where the casing line will be so that you can draw the shade into the ballerina waist shape. Trim the cylinder so that there is sufficient fabric left to make the elastic casing.

6 Make another shorter and smaller cylinder shape in the same manner to fit the top of the shade. This is also drawn in with elastic through a casing edge.

7 Place the shades over the wire form, thread the elastic through and draw it up in the casing pockets. The bottom shade should overlap the top shade. Pin the lower edge to the wire form and stitch in place evenly around the edge. Do the same for the top of the shade. A folded and pressed piece of fabric has been wound around the shade at the waist section to camouflage the elastic.

HANDY HINT

Silk ribbon embroidery is by nature quite messy on the back. It is a dimensional thread and it is impossible to keep the back of the work as neat as the front. It is important to be neat when working this project because light will shine through the fabrics when the lamp is in use. Avoid looping threads from one flower to the next. Instead, begin and end at each flower as this will help to keep the back of your work neat. This is particularly important if you are using dark-coloured ribbons or threads.

Blooming Baskets
– A Garden Landscape

This charming garden landscape features a wrought iron planter pole with hanging baskets of geraniums. A profusion of blooms at the base add to the visual interest and increases the sense of perspective in the embroidery. The background has been hand painted, using several colours to achieve greater depth. The colours of the flowers could easily be altered to give this embroidery a totally different appearance. Two whimsical butterflies add further interest.

REQUIREMENTS

Cotton natural-seeded homespun fabric, 30cm (12") square.

Water erasable pen.

Sharp lead pencil.

Decoart Americana folk art paint DA68 (Slate grey), DA52 (Avocado), DA59 (Toffee).

Ribbons and threads as listed below.

Embroidery hoop.

1 Daffodils

Component	Thread	No.	Colour	Stitch Used
Leaves	2mm silk	32	Light blue-green	Extended/ couched ribbon stitch
Trumpet	4mm silk	15	Bright yellow	Loop
Petals	2mm silk	13	Pale lemon	Ribbon
Buds	4mm silk	15	Bright yellow	Ribbon
Stems/details	Rajmahal	805	Sassafras	Fly/straight

2 Grape Hyacinths

Component	Thread	No.	Colour	Stitch Used
Leaves	4mm silk	171	Medium olive green	Extended/ couched ribbon stitch
Stems	Rajmahal	421	Green earth	Stem
Flowers	4mm silk	102	Deep mauve	French knots

3 Foxgloves

Component	Thread	No.	Colour	Stitch Used
Stems	Rajmahal	805	Sassafras	Stem
Flowers	4mm silk	46	Dark sky blue	French knots and ribbon stitch
	4mm silk	45	Medium sky blue	French knots and ribbon stitch
	4mm silk	125	Light blue	French knots and ribbon stitch
Leaves	4mm silk	33	Medium blue-green	Extended ribbon stitch

4 Blue Dutch Hyacinths

Component	Thread	No.	Colour	Stitch Used
Leaves	4mm silk	72	Dark jungle green	Extended/ couched ribbon stitch
Stems	Rajmahal	421	Green earth	Stem
Flowers	4mm silk	44	Medium sky blue	French knots

5 Flowering Foliage

Component	Thread	No.	Colour	Stitch Used
Stems	Rajmahal	421	Green earth	Stem
Leaves	4mm silk	62	Light ice green	Ribbon
Flowers	4mm silk	157	Very light dusky pink	French knots

ENLARGE AT 110% ON
A PHOTOCOPIER

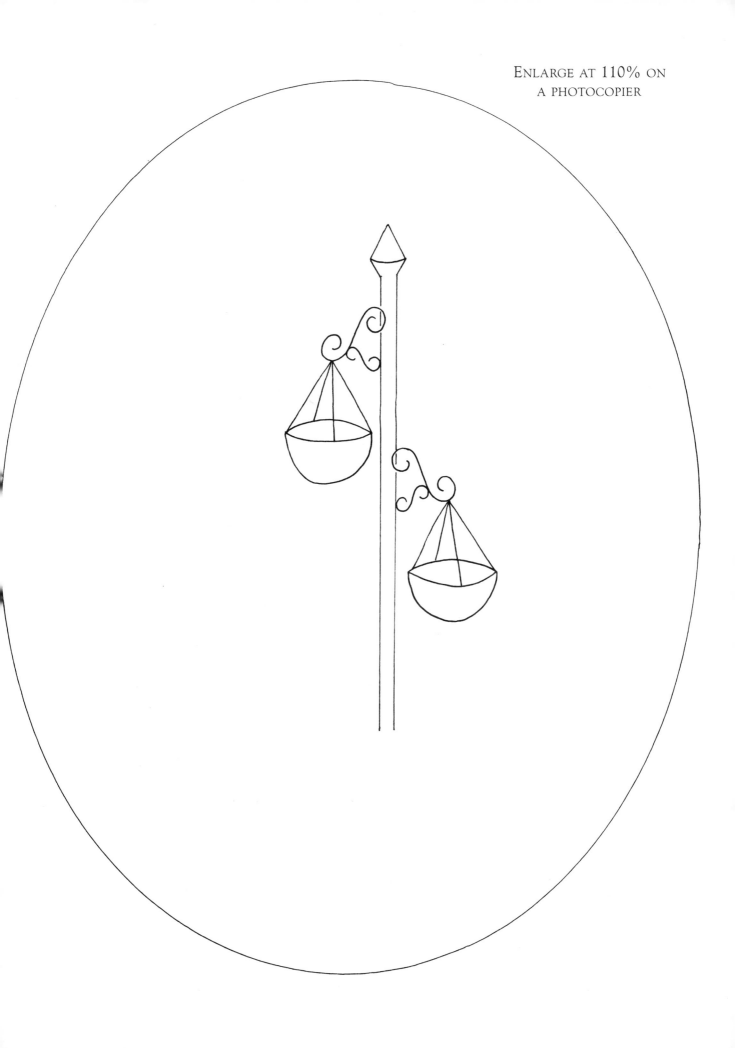

6 Lavender

Component	Thread	No.	Colour	Stitch Used
Stems	Rajmahal	805	Sassafras	Stem
Flowers	4mm silk	178	Light grape	French knots
Flowers	4mm silk	179	Medium grape	French knots
Leaves	4mm silk	33	Medium blue-green	Ribbon

7 Background Foliage (RHS)

Component	Thread	No.	Colour	Stitch Used
Stems	Rajmahal	521	Maidenhair	Stem
Leaves	4mm silk	155	Palest green	Ribbon

8 Pink Daisies

Component	Thread	No.	Colour	Stitch Used
Stems	Rajmahal	421	Green earth	Stem
Flower centres	4mm silk	15	Bright yellow	French knots
Flower petals	4mm silk	157	Very light dusky pink	Ribbon
Leaves	2mm silk	20	Medium grass green	Ribbon

9 Freesias

Component	Thread	No.	Colour	Stitch Used
Stems	Rajmahal	521	Maidenhair	Stem
Flowers	4mm silk	13	Pale lemon	French knots and ribbon stitch
Leaves	2mm silk	21	Dark forest green	Extended/ couched ribbon stitch

10 Violets

Component	Thread	No.	Colour	Stitch Used
Flower centres	4mm silk	15	Bright yellow	French knots
Flower petals	4mm silk	84	Purple	Ribbon
Leaves	7mm silk	20	Medium grass green	Ribbon

11 Forget-me-nots

Component	Thread	No.	Colour	Stitch Used
Flower centres	4mm silk	15	Bright yellow	French knots
Flowers	4mm silk	157	Very light dusky pink	French knots
Leaves	4mm silk	31	Light apple green	Ribbon

12 Geranium Basket (Light Pink)

Component	Thread	No.	Colour	Stitch Used
Stems	Rajmahal	421	Green earth	Stem
Flowers	4mm silk	112	Light rose pink	French knots
Leaves	4mm silk	20	Medium grass green	Ribbon

13 Geranium Basket (Dark Pink)

Component	Thread	No.	Colour	Stitch Used
Stems	Rajmahal	421	Green earth	Stem
Flowers	4mm silk	11	Deep rose pink	French knots
Leaves	4mm silk	72	Dark forest green	Ribbon

14 Background Foliage (LHS)

Component	Thread	No.	Colour	Stitch Used
Stems	Rajmahal	311	Fresco oil	Stem
Leaves	4mm silk	66	Light brown	Ribbon
Additional leaves	9mm	56	Spark Organdy ribbon	Loose ribbon stitch

15 Butterflies

Component	Thread	No.	Colour	Stitch Used
Head and body	Rajmahal	226	Gothic grey	French knot and stem
Antennae	Rajmahal	29	Charcoal	Pistil
Wings	9mm	37	Spark Organdy ribbon	Loose ribbon stitch

METHOD

1   Using a water erasable pen, mark the oval shape on the fabric. Place the feature positioning diagram beneath the fabric and, using a sharp lead pencil and a very light touch, trace over the planter support post. The stem stitch will cover these pencil marks later.

2   Mix the paints with water. Paint the post first, the baskets second and the green areas next. Lastly, colour the sky area very lightly. Make sure you allow each colour to dry before starting on the next.

3   Stem stitch over the post outline and the chains which support the baskets using 1 strand of Rajmahal thread 226 (Gothic grey). Embroider the flowers in the order given above so that some can be worked over the top of others to add dimension and depth.

4   If required, include a tiny spider web and spider. The spider web is worked in 1 strand of silver Madeira metallic thread and straight stitches only. The spider is a single wrap French knot with 2 strands of Rajmahal thread 29 (Charcoal).

5   Remove any visible marks from the water erasable pen using a cotton bud dipped in cold water.

6   Choose a complementary frame to display your work.

HANDY HINT

Spark Organdy, a sheer nylon ribbon available in a variety of colours and widths, has been used to maximum effect in this embroidery to further enhance the sense of depth. It covers areas quickly and, because it is sheer, the stems etc. appear through the ribbon.

DOILEY STORAGE SACHET

SHHH! THE FAIRIES ARE HOME — A BLANKET

Shhh! The Fairies Are Home — A Blanket (Detail)

Doiley Storage Sachet (Detail)

Doiley
Storage Sachet

T his superb garden landscape has been worked on pure Dupion silk which has been made into an old-fashioned doiley storage sachet. These were used in Victorian times to store doilies neatly in the linen cupboard to ensure that they were ready for use when required. The design features a hand-painted background which increases the depth in the embroidery and adds to the perspective achieved with the silk ribbon stitching. It would also be suitable for framing.

REQUIREMENTS

Ivory Dupion silk, 75cm x 115cm (30" x 46").

Iron-on flexible interfacing, such as Whisperweft or Armorweft.

.01 pigma pen (Sepia Brown).

Water erasable pen.

Decoart Americana acrylic folk art paints DA3 (Buttermilk), DA59 (Toffee), DA52 (Avocado), DA152 (Shale Green).

Bristle brush.

Silk ribbons and threads as listed below.

Embroidery hoop.

Fabric marking pen.

4 circles of heavy cardboard, each 29cm (11½") in diameter.

PVA glue.

Thin wadding to pad the embroidery.

Bias cut silk for piping cord.

Satin-edged silk georgette ribbon to form the hinge and the bow.

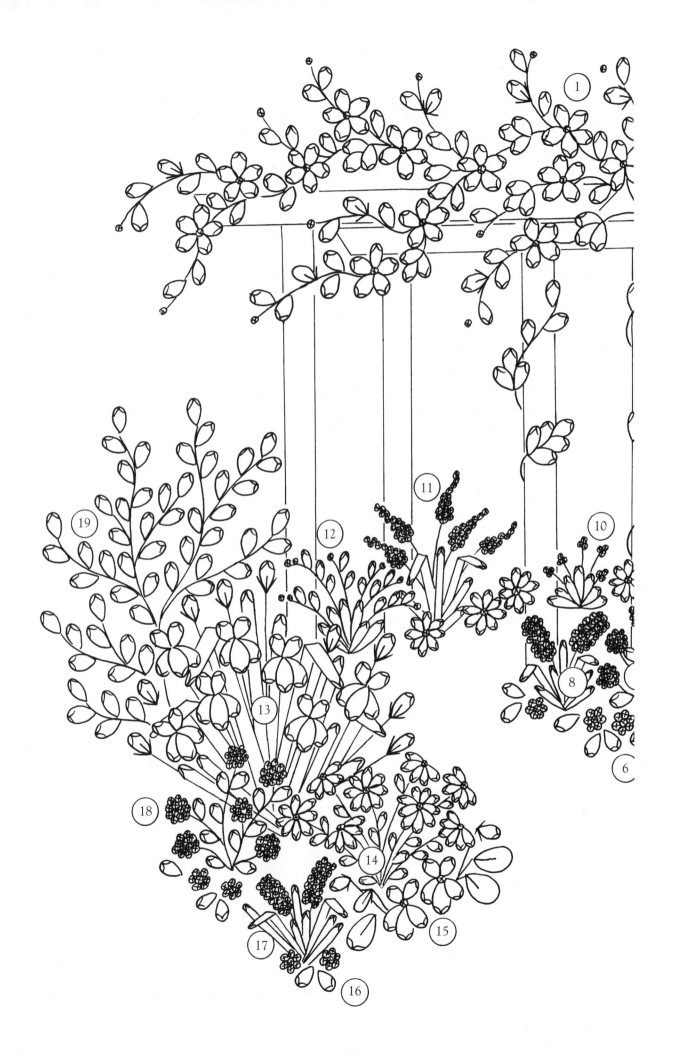

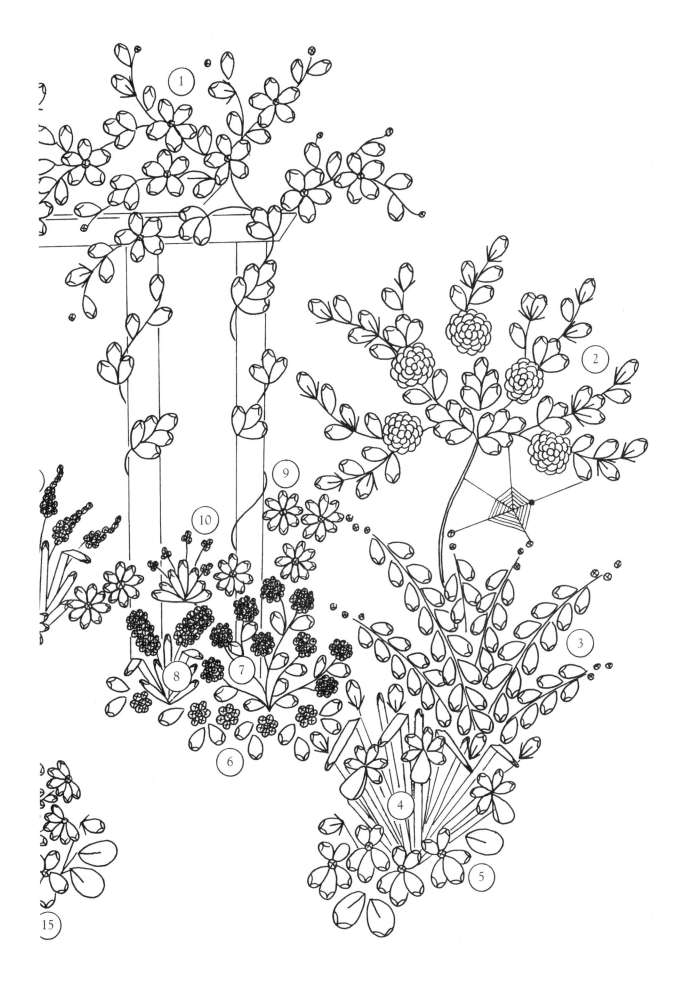

1 Climbing Vine — Allamanda

Component	Thread	No.	Colour	Stitch Used
Stems	Rajmahal	521	Maidenhair	Stem
Flower centres	4mm silk	15	Bright yellow	French knots
Flower petals	4mm silk	13	Pale lemon	Ribbon
Flower buds	4mm silk	13	Pale lemon	Ribbon
Bud details	Rajmahal	521	Maidenhair	Fly/straight
Leaves	4mm silk	20	Medium grass green	Ribbon

2 Standard Rose

Component	Thread	No.	Colour	Stitch Used
Stem	Rajmahal	521	Maidenhair	Stem stitch
Roses	4mm silk	5	Very pale pink	Spider web/ woven rose
Buds	4mm silk	5	Very pale pink	Ribbon
Bud details	Rajmahal	521	Maidenhair	Fly/straight
Leaves	4mm silk	72	Dark jungle green	Ribbon

3 Foxgloves

Component	Thread	No.	Colour	Stitch Used
Stems	Rajmahal	805	Sassafras	Stem
Flowers	4mm silk	45	Dark sky blue	French knots and ribbon stitch
	4mm silk	44	Medium sky blue	French knots and ribbon stitch
	4mm silk	125	Light blue	French knots and ribbon stitch

4 Daffodils

Component	Thread	No.	Colour	Stitch Used
Leaves	2mm silk	33	Medium blue green	Extended/ couched ribbon stitch
Trumpet	4mm silk	15	Bright yellow	Loop
Petals	2mm silk	13	Pale lemon	Ribbon
Buds	4mm silk	15	Bright yellow	Ribbon
Stems/details	Rajmahal	805	Sassafras	Fly/straight

5 Violets

Component	Thread	No.	Colour	Stitch Used
Centres	4mm silk	15	Bright yellow	French knots
Petals/buds	4mm silk	84	Purple	Ribbon
Stems	Rajmahal	521	Maidenhair	Fly/straight
Leaves	7mm silk	20	Medium grass green	Ribbon

6 Forget-me-nots

Component	Thread	No.	Colour	Stitch Used
Petals	4mm silk	125	Light blue	French knots
Centres	4mm silk	15	Bright yellow	French knot
Leaves	4mm silk	31	Light apple green	Ribbon

7 Geranium

Component	Thread	No.	Colour	Stitch Used
Stems	Rajmahal	521	Maidenhair	Stem
Flowers	4mm silk	158	Medium dusky pink	French knots
Leaves	4mm silk	72	Dark jungle green	Ribbon

8 White Dutch Hyacinths

Component	Thread	No.	Colour	Stitch Used
Stems	Rajmahal	521	Maidenhair	Stem
Leaves	2mm silk	21	Dark forest green	Extended/couched ribbon stitch
Flowers	4mm silk	3	White	French knots

9 Groundcover Flowers

Component	Thread	No.	Colour	Stitch Used
Centres	4mm silk	15	Bright yellow	French knots
Petals	2mm silk	3	White	Ribbon
	2mm silk	13	Pale lemon	Ribbon
	2mm silk	163	Very light rose pink	Ribbon

10 Dianthus

Component	Thread	No.	Colour	Stitch Used
Stems	Rajmahal	521	Maidenhair	Stem
Leaves	2mm silk	20	Medium grass green	Extended ribbon stitch
Flowers	4mm silk	125	Light blue	French knots

11. Grape Hyacinths

Component	Thread	No.	Colour	Stitch Used
Stems	Rajmahal	521	Maidenhair	Stem
Leaves	2mm silk	20	Medium grass green	Extended/ couched ribbon stitch
Flowers	4mm silk	102	Deep mauve	French knots

12 Freesias

Component	Thread	No.	Colour	Stitch Used
Stems	Rajmahal	521	Maidenhair	Stem
Leaves	2mm silk	21	Dark forest green	Extended ribbon stitch
Flowers	2mm silk	13	Pale lemon	French knots and ribbon stitch

13 Iris

Component	Thread	No.	Colour	Stitch Used
Leaves	4mm silk	32	Light blue-green	Extended/ couched ribbon stitch
Flowers/buds	4mm silk	178	Light grape	Ribbon
	4mm silk	117	Light blue-mauve	Ribbon
	4mm silk	22	Light mauve	Ribbon
Stems/details	Rajmahal	805	Sassafras	Fly/straight

14 White Daisies

Component	Thread	No.	Colour	Stitch Used
Stems	Rajmahal	521	Maidenhair	Stem
Flower centres	4mm silk	15	Bright yellow	French knots
Flower petals	2mm silk	3	White	Ribbon
Leaves	2mm silk	21	Dark forest green	Ribbon

15 Violets

As for those worked in 5.

16 Forget-me-nots

As for those worked in 6.

17 Lemon Dutch Hyacinth

Component	Thread	No.	Colour	Stitch Used
Stems	Rajmahal	521	Maidenhair	Stem
Leaves	2mm silk	21	Dark forest green	Extended/ couched ribbon stitch
Flowers	4mm silk	13	Pale lemon	French knots

18 Geranium

As for those worked in 7.

19 Background Foliage

Component	Thread	No.	Colour	Stitch Used
Stems	Rajmahal	521	Maidenhair	Stem
Leaves	4mm silk	171	Medium olive green	Ribbon

METHOD

1   Cut the silk 6cm (2½") larger than the overall design. Iron on the interfacing to the back of the silk. Overlock all the edges to prevent fraying.

2   Using the flower positioning diagram, mark in the pergola with the pigma pen and the edge of the path with the water erasable pen.

3   Water down the paints (see 'Painted Backgrounds') and carefully fill in the pergola timberwork using DA3 (Buttermilk). Paint the path in this colour also, using horizontal brushstrokes, and add highlights in DA59 (Toffee) for additional interest. Allow these sections to dry completely. Referring to the position of the flowers in the flower positioning diagram and using both shades of green, create a background for the embroidered flowers using a stabbing action with the bristle brush. Ensure that the darker colour is used in the foreground

of the work and that the lighter shade is reserved for the background of the design. Allow the paint to dry.

4   With a fabric marking pen, mark the stem lines. Then, following the guide above and referring to the flower positioning diagram, stitch all the flower groups in position. You will find it easier to work in the order suggested.

5   If you wish, add the spider web and spider, using 1 strand of silver Madeira metallic thread and straight stitches only for the web and a single wrap French knot with 2 strands of Rajmahal thread 29 (Charcoal) for the spider.

6   Once the embroidery is complete, remove any visible marks of the fabric marking pen using a cotton bud dipped in cold water. Allow to dry completely.

7   Glue thin wadding to 2 of the cardboard circles on one side only. All 4 circles have to be covered with silk but only the outer ones are padded. One of the outer circles is covered with the embroidered piece of fabric. To achieve a smooth edge, clip the silk close to the cardboard and, using PVA glue to hold it in place, stretch the clipped edges over the cardboard and smooth into position. Allow the glue to dry. Make a silk piping cord from bias cut silk to give the circles a more tailored appearance. Glue this to the outer circles at this point. The ribbon hinge and the two lengths of ribbon which will form the bow are now glued into position. The inner circles are then glued to the outer circles to form the sandwich and to hide the clipped edges of silk.

8   Weight the edges of the sachet, avoiding the embroidery so that it will remain flat and not buckle during the glueing process.

HANDY HINT

It is always much easier to draw fabric around a circle or curve of cardboard if the edges are clipped quite close to the cardboard, but not too close or the cuts will be visible. The clips should also be quite close together as this will help to keep the edge neat.

Shhh!
The Fairies
Are Home
—A Blanket

A delightful baby's cot blanket with a fairytale theme as the central design, it features two toadstool homes, surrounded by a colourful cottage garden, presumably where the fairies live. The fairies must be home because the lights are on in the upstairs windows. Tiny bees spell the name of the project amongst the flowers in one corner and similar flowers decorate the other.

REQUIREMENTS

1 cot size blanket, approximately 120cm x 80cm (4' x 2' 8").

Tulle.

Black permanent marking pen.

Water-erasable fabric marking pen.

Ribbons and threads as listed below.

Decoart Americana acrylic folk art paint, DA52 (Avocado), DA59 (Toffee), DA3 (Buttermilk).

Decoart fabric painting medium, DAS10.

Bristle or deersfoot brush.

Red bias satin piping, approximately 4.5m (14') long.

Backing fabric, approximately 1.5m (4½') (The one used had an all-over small leaf print in antique white, designed to tone with the blanket.).

Large embroidery hoop.

The flowers are listed as they appear on the blanket (from left to right).

1 Geranium

Component	Thread	No.	Colour	Stitch Used
Stems	Rajmahal	521	Maidenhair	Stem
Flowers	4mm silk	157	Very light dusky pink	French knots
Leaves	4mm silk	72	Dark jungle green	Ribbon

2 Lily of the Valley

Component	Thread	No.	Colour	Stitch Used
Stems	Rajmahal	521	Maidenhair	Stem
Leaves	2mm silk	21	Dark forest green	Extended/ couched ribbon stitch
Flowers	4mm silk	3	White	French knots

3 Pale Blue Forget-me-nots

Component	Thread	No.	Colour	Stitch Used
Centres	4mm silk	15	Bright yellow	French knot
Petals	4mm silk	125	Light blue	French knots
Leaves	4mm silk	31	Light apple green	Ribbon

4 Grape Hyacinths

Component	Thread	No.	Colour	Stitch Used
Stems	Rajmahal	521	Maidenhair	Stem
Leaves	2mm silk	20	Medium grass green	Extended ribbon stitch
Flowers	4mm silk	23	Deep mauve	French knots

LEFT HAND SIDE

MIDDLE

EMBROIDERY DESIGN
FOR LOWER RIGHT
HAND CORNER
(LEFT HALF)

The fairies are home

EMBROIDERY DESIGN
FOR LOWER RIGHT
HAND CORNER
(RIGHT HALF)

EMBROIDERY DESIGN
FOR LOWER LEFT
HAND CORNER

5 Foxgloves

Component	Thread	No.	Colour	Stitch Used
Stems	Rajmahal	805	Sassafras	Stem
Flowers	4mm silk	46	Dark sky blue	French knot and ribbon stitch
	4mm silk	125	Light blue	French knot and ribbon stitch
	4mm silk	90	Very pale sky blue	French knot and ribbon stitch
Leaves	4mm silk	33	Medium blue green	Extended ribbon stitch

6 Pink Forget-me-nots

Component	Thread	No.	Colour	Stitch Used
Centres	4mm silk	15	Bright yellow	French knot
Flower petals	4mm silk	157	Very light dusky pink	French knots
Leaves	4mm silk	31	Light apple green	Ribbon

7 Lemon Hyacinths

Component	Thread	No.	Colour	Stitch Used
Stems	Rajmahal	521	Maidenhair	Stem
Flowers	4mm silk	13	Pale lemon	French knots
Leaves	2mm silk	21	Dark forest green	Extended ribbon stitch

8 Toadstools

Component	Thread	No.	Colour	Stitch Used
Roof	Gumnut 2 ply crewel wool	039	Red	Stem stitch outline
		991	White	filled in with French knots
Stem	Gumnut 2 ply crewel wool	963		Stem
Ribs	Rajmahal	226	Gothic grey	Stem
Windows/door	Rajmahal	171	Woodlands	Stem
Light in window	Rajmahal	45	Baby camel	Straight
Doorknob	Rajmahal	29	Charcoal	French knot
Chimney	Rajmahal	226	Charcoal	Stem/straight
Chimney stack	Rajmahal	171	Woodlands	Stem

9 Yellow Daisies between Toadstools

Component	Thread	No.	Colour	Stitch Used
Stems	Rajmahal	521	Maidenhair	Stem
Flower centres	4mm silk	3	White	French knot
Flower petals	4mm silk	15	Bright yellow	Ribbon

10 Pale Blue Forget-me-nots
Worked as for those detailed in 3.

11 Grape Hyacinths
Worked as for those detailed in 4.

12 Pale Lemon Daisies

Component	Thread	No.	Colour	Stitch Used
Stems	Rajmahal	521	Maidenhair	Stem
Flower centres	4mm silk	15	Bright yellow	French knot
Flower petals	4mm silk	13	Pale lemon	Ribbon

13 Pink Forget-me-nots

Worked as for those detailed in 6.

14 Lavender

Component	Thread	No.	Colour	Stitch Used
Stems	Rajmahal	805	Sassafras	Stem
Flowers	4mm silk	179	Medium grape	French knots
	4mm silk	23	Deep mauve	French knots
Leaves	2mm silk	33	Medium blue green	Ribbon

15 Blue Hyacinths

Component	Thread	No.	Colour	Stitch Used
Stems	Rajmahal	521	Maidenhair	Stem
Flowers	4mm silk	46	Dark sky blue	French knots
Leaves	2mm silk	21	Dark forest green	Extended ribbon stitch

16 Mailbox

Component	Thread	No.	Colour	Stitch Used
Post/lid	Rajmahal	171	Woodlands	Stem
Box	Rajmahal	226	Gothic grey	Stem

17 Daisies near Mailbox

Component	Thread	No.	Colour	Stitch Used
Stem	Rajmahal	521	Maidenhair	Stem
Flower centres	4mm silk	15	Bright yellow	French knot
Flower petals	4mm silk	90	Very pale sky blue	Ribbon
Leaves	2mm silk	20	Medium grass green	Ribbon

18 Garden Creatures

BEES

Component	Thread	No.	Colour	Stitch Used
Body	4mm silk	15	Bright yellow	Ribbon
Details/ stripes	Rajmahal	29	Charcoal	French knots/straight stitch
Wings	2mm silk	13	Pale lemon	

BUTTERFLIES

Component	Thread	No.	Colour	Stitch Used
Body	Rajmahal	226	Gothic grey	Stem
Antennae	Rajmahal	29	Charcoal	Pistil
Wings	9mm Spark Organdy		Mauve	Ribbon

INCH WORM

Component	Thread	No.	Colour	Stitch Used
Body	4mm silk	65	Light caramel	French knots
Segments	Rajmahal	171	Woodlands	Straight

SPIDER WEB AND SPIDER

Component	Thread	No.	Colour	Stitch Used
Web	Madeira		Silver	Straight
Spider	Rajmahal	29	Charcoal	Single wrap French knot, 2 strands

19 Anemones and Ranunculus

Scattered throughout the design and used to fill in any remaining spaces, each of these flowers has eight petals.

Component	Thread	No.	Colour	Stitch Used
Flower centres	Rajmahal	29	Charcoal	French knot
Petals	2mm silk	157	Very light dusky pink	Ribbon
	2mm silk	13	Pale lemon	
	2mm silk	15	Bright yellow	
	2mm silk	23	Deep mauve	
	2mm silk	179	Medium grape	
	2mm silk	50	Rich deep red	

METHOD

1   Place the piece of tulle over the main design and, using the permanent marking pen, trace around the outline of the toadstools. In addition, mark the stems of the major flower groups (this will give you an indication of the extent of the painted background) and the broken centre lines shown on the pattern sheet. Leave pen markings to dry.

2   Determine the centre of your blanket by folding it in quarters. Mark the central point with a pin. Unfold the blanket and carefully pin the tulle pattern onto the blanket, matching the centre marks. Using the water erasable pen, trace over the pattern outline through the tulle. This will result in a dotted line which you can retrace and darken once the tulle is removed.

3   Work the outlines of the toadstools and the mailbox using the threads and stitches listed above. The painted background is applied at this stage to provide a background for the flowers.

4   Place a very small amount of each of the paints onto separate saucers. Mix the correct quantity of textile medium with each lot of paint, according to the manufacturer's instructions, until well combined. Then mix some water with a smaller amount of DA52 (Avocado) to create a watercolour-type wash. Apply to the blanket with the bristle brush using a stabbing technique. The wash of colour is built up gradually on the blanketing where the flowers are to be embroidered. Be very careful not to apply it too heavily. Remember that it is only a background wash. Allow to dry completely. The two colours used for the path, DA59 (Toffee) and DA3 (Buttermilk), can then be watered down and applied in the same manner, building up the tone differences by applying the darker colour over the lighter one. Take care to keep the outlines of the painted areas quite irregular as this will give your work a more natural look. Once again, allow to dry. The paint needs to be set once it is dry by ironing for approximately 20–30 seconds in each area. Place a clean cloth over the paint before applying the iron to the blanket for the required time (see manufacturer's instructions). The major stems of the flower groups can be redrawn at this stage using the tulle pattern.

5   The toadstools are then simply filled in using 1 strand of the 2 ply wool and single wrap French knots. The details on the toadstools can also be worked in the Rajmahal threads and stitches listed.

6   Work all the major flower groups according to the above charts and then fill in the spaces with single anemones and ranunculus in the colours indicated. The stitch guide and the illustrations will be of assistance if you are unfamiliar with the stitches used. A single strand of the threads mentioned has been used throughout the project, except for the spider which can be added with the web at this stage, if required.

7   Transfer the corner designs using the same method as described above. Work as detailed in the charts. The writing and the flight of the bees is worked in back stitch and running stitch using a single strand of Rajmahal 226 (Gothic grey). The leaves of the anemones and ranunculus as they appear in the corners are worked in 4mm silk, 31 (Light apple green).

8   Once the embroidery is complete, ensure that there are no visible marks left from the water erasable pen. To remove marks, simply dab them with a cotton bud dipped in cold water and allow the blanket to air dry.

9   The satin piping is either hand or machine stitched to the blanket approximately 6cm in from the edge, overlapping at the corners. The blanket is backed with a prewashed cotton fabric which is simply brought around to meet the piping with mitred corners. The backing fabric is hand stitched into place at the mitred corners and along the edges.

HANDY HINT

Pin the backing fabric in place around the entire blanket prior to stitching. This enables adjustment, if required, to the width of the edges and corners, ensuring that they will be as neat as possible once they have been stitched.

Stockists

SILK RIBBONS

Cotton on Creations
Suite 107
2 Pembroke Street
Epping NSW 2121
Australia

Phone (02) 9868 4583 Fax (02) 9868 4269

(Wholesalers only, but they may be able to help you find a local stockist if you have difficulty locating colours.)

OVERDYED OR HAND-DYED SILK RIBBONS

Colour Streams
88 Balaka Drive
Carlingford NSW 2118
Australia

Phone & Fax (02) 9871 4422

Glenlorin
PO Box 974
Pennant Hills NSW 1715

Phone (02) 9980 1993

Petals Australia
PO Box 657
Nambour QLD 4560

Phone (07) 5441 5797 Fax (07) 5441 5697

STRANDED ART SILK

Rajmahal
1 Anderson Street
Bendigo VIC 3550
Australia

Phone (03) 5441 7787 Fax (03) 5441 7959

(Stranded silk is available at many leading craft shops, but if you have difficulty locating it, Rajmahal will be able to give you details of your local stockists.)

Don't overlook your local embroidery guild or sewing interest group for information to help you obtain the supplies you require. Many of their members have years of sewing and embroidery experience and a wealth of knowledge on sourcing materials.